STORYTELLING
the disciple making path

LEADERS' NOTES can be found at the rear of the book.
All Scripture quotations, unless otherwise indicated, are from The Holy Bible, New International Version (NIV) Copyright 1973, 1978, 1984, 2011, by Biblica, Inc. Used by permission. All rights reserved worldwide. Any online content (websites, YouTube videos, or blogs) in this Bible study material are only presented as a resource.

Matthews, Phillip G. (author)
Storytelling, the Disciple Making Path – Second Edition
16 Studies for Individuals or Groups
ISBN 978-1-923333-18-5 (paperback)
ISBN 978-1-923386-08-2 (eBook)
Bible Study Guide

Copyedited by Dr Ross James – Author of
Ascent, Crest, Perspective: The making of a bamboo camel
Proofread by Natalie Matthews

Bulk purchases for retail book shops, ministries or churches may be obtained.
For information, please email
sales.storytellingthedmp@gmail.com

Typeset Minion Pro 11/15
Cover and book design by Green Hill Publishing

16 Studies for
Individuals
or Groups

STORY†ELLING

the disciple making path

PHILLIP G. MATTHEWS

CONTENTS

AUTHOR

PHILLIP GREGORY MATTHEWS (B.MIN, GRAD DIP.MIN, M.A.) has been a disciple of Jesus for 40 years. He lives in Perth, Western Australia, and has worked as a horticulturist, arboricultural consultant, pastor, aged-care chaplain, and a Bible study leader. Phillip says this background has given him the skills to cultivate, sow, water, feed and grow not only plants, but also people as they embark on a disciple making path by studying the Bible, disciple making and Jesus' story.

But something changed when he used *The NIV Harmony of the Gospels* (published by *HarperCollins*) to study the life of Christ chronologically; from birth to death, his resurrection and ascension. Because the disciple making path became so clear, Phillip was compelled to walk along it as Jesus did, and to bring as many other people as possible with him.

That led Phillip to develop Storytelling Jesus' Story, a process that he uses for his personal devotions and to lead Bible study groups. Videos storytelling Jesus' story have reached many people through online platforms (Facebook and YouTube).

Storytelling the Disciple Making Path has 16 devotional Bible study guides that can be used in small groups. However, people can use this material in their personal devotions and be equipped to build up others, one-on-one in everyday conversations, using the Storytelling Jesus' Story process.

DEDICATION

TO MY WIFE, NATALIE, AND OUR TWO ADULT CHILDREN, Sharon and John, who have supported the crazy ideas I had about disciple making. Even when I thought these ideas may not work, you prayed, encouraged and were there for me.

To my mother, Robyn, who encouraged me to go to church and youth group, throughout my childhood and teenage years, where I learnt that Jesus loves me, because the Bible told me so.

I also thank the pastors, ministers, Bible college lecturers and mentors, Steve Schoof, Colin Lituri, Matthew Munn, Michael Parsons, Brian Harris, Mark Wilson, John North, Aaron Daniell, Monica O'Neil, Karen Siggins, the late Ian Fauchon and many others who helped me to grow from spiritual infancy to spiritual maturity as a disciple maker who continues to make disciples for Jesus. And a big thank you to Ross James, whose editorial expertise smoothed out a rough diamond.

Also, I would like to dedicate this Bible study guide to the glory of God, for the progress of disciple making among your people, worldwide, because this book is for you. Thank you, Jesus.

ACKNOWLEDGMENTS

I WOULD LIKE TO ACKNOWLEDGE PASTOR COLLIN AND Pastor Matthew (the previous pastors at Woodvale Baptist Church in WA) for introducing the idea of disciple making. Also, John North from Ambassadors for Christ International-Australia and his teaching at SHIFTm2M seminars. John gave me two books, *Knowing Him* and *The NIV Harmony of the Gospels*. Using *The Harmony of the Gospels*, I explored the life of Christ chronologically, from birth to ascension. This study of the disciple making path as documented in the four gospels of Matthew, Mark, Luke and John was so clear, I was compelled to walk along it.

I had always struggled with evangelism, but when it was placed into the disciple making context, it all came together for me. I had studied for years at Bible colleges, earning a bachelor's degree in ministry, and was part way through studying for a master's degree in Bible studies. And yet, in all that time at Bible college, there was never a unit on disciple making.

Another book that opened wide the disciple making path was *DiscipleShift: Five steps That Help your Church make Disciples who make Disciples* (Zondervan). I thank the authors, J. Putman and B. Harrington for their work.

Sam Chan opened the huge idea of storytelling Jesus' story through his book, *Evangelism in a Skeptical World: How to Make the Unbelievable News About Jesus More Believable* (Zondervan) for which I am thankful.

I owe a grateful thanks to a weekly home group that I led with people who joined me on the disciple making ride of our lives. I thank Ken, Lynita, Asha, Lothar and Natalie for being my core go-to-people. Thank you for challenging me, working through, and accepting some of the ideas we examined as we learnt to re-tell some of Jesus' stories.

A big thank you for all the prayer partnerships involved in the Storytelling Jesus' Story WhatsApp group, who were encouraged and inspired about the crazy idea of storytelling Jesus' stories.

COMMON ACRONYMS

Acts	The Acts of the Apostles	**Hb**	Hebrew language
AD	Anno Domini (Latin, the year of our Lord)	**Heb**	Hebrews (Letter to)
BC	Before Christ	**Hos**	Hosea
Cf.	Compare or confer	**Isa**	Isaiah
1 Chr	1 Chronicles	**Jer**	Jeremiah
2 Chr	2 Chronicles	**Jud**	Jude
Col	Colossians	**Jms**	James
1 Cor	1 Corinthians	**Jn**	Gospel According to John
2 Cor	2 Corinthians	**1Jn**	1 John
CSB	Christian Standard Bible.	**1 Kgs**	1 Kings
Dan	Daniel	**2 Kgs**	2 Kings
Deut	Deuteronomy	**Lat**	Latin
Ecc	Ecclesiastes	**Lev**	Leviticus
CEB	Common English Bible	**Lk**	Gospel According to Luke
Etc	Etcetera, Latin for "and so on"	**Mal**	Malachi
Eph	Ephesians	**MEV**	Modern English Version
ERV	Easy-to-Read Version	**Mic**	Micah
Ex	Exodus	**Mk**	Gospel According to Mark
Ezek	Ezekiel	**MSG**	The Message Bible
Gal	Galatians	**Mt**	Gospel According to Matthew
Gen	Genesis	**Neh**	Nehemiah
Gk	Greek language	**NET**	New English Translation

INTRODUCTION

THERE ARE MORE THAN A FEW BOOKS ON DISCIPLE making to choose from. What then could conceivably warrant adding one more to an already well-stocked bookshelf? Those who contributed to this book are not under the delusion that its contents will change the world, but we hope it would change your world. We truly believe that the time is ripe for a new kind of Bible study material that combines an awakening hunger for disciple making in church small groups with the passionate commitment of disciples who make disciples who, in turn make other disciples.

This is done with convincing, connecting and compelling stories from the life of our Lord Jesus Christ. We present this material not as a book, but as a 16 study disciple-making Bible guide that is easily understood and applied. Disciple making has been so unpretentious and quiet that the average Christian believer hardly hears of it. How can that be?

In recent years, churches have declined in numbers and—even more alarming—Christians have become somewhat marginalised in their workplaces, social activities and communities. They see and experience a community that is growing and moving faster than their church (Moran, 2014). An indicator of dramatic change is that 50 years ago, most people had some knowledge of the Bible, yet biblical illiteracy characterises many people today.

When we share the truth of our faith to people in our workplaces and community, it feels like we are living in different worlds.

Today's society sees the Church and Christians as unloving, judgmental and critical, or—and even worse—insincere and phony. They see the Church and Christians as a part of a problem, not the solution. Perhaps they would say of the handful of Christians they did know, "Well, they are OK" (Kimball, 2008, p.13). Now however, they increasingly regard Christians as the bad guys. To be a good person, it seems, the Christian is expected to compromise with the current culture, whereas the Bible reveals another way (McAlpine, 2022, p. 11).

Some churches know that they are not perfect (but Jesus is) and nor are they the solution (but Jesus is) yet they are growing numerically (Matthews, 2007). However, just because a person attends church, it does not necessarily mean they understand what a disciple of Jesus really is, nor the importance of growing towards spiritual maturity. The evidence, perhaps, is that the rates of divorce, addiction, and spending habits among Christians are only slightly lower than unbelievers (FactChecker: *Divorce Rate Among Christians - The Gospel Coalition*, 2012, Sep 25).

Our attempts at personal and public evangelism seem to produce few conversions or none. We quote Scriptures like John 3:16. We ask questions: "If you die tonight, do you know you would go to heaven?" (Kennedy, 1983, p. 16). "Have you heard about Jesus?" "Did you know he died for sinners?" Even when we pray and acknowledge the leading of the Holy Spirit, it seems impossible to merely talk someone into God's family.

These approaches have a defective idea of spiritual maturity. Growing spiritually in one's walk with God requires more than simply receiving spiritual knowledge. Jesus ensured that his disciples were fully trained disciples under a balanced, biblical ministry that saw them mature spiritually as disciples who made other disciples. Jesus devoted a great deal of time to being alone with his disciples, strengthening their faith as he trained them for ministry (Mk 9:30). He frequently chose to focus on training rather than evangelism, particularly as the crowds increased, knowing his time was brief.

Here we must recognise the need for a balance between evangelism and discipleship. As important as evangelism is, it is only one part of our mission. We are to make disciples, not just converts (Spader, 2012, p. 29).

Equally, if we focus on discipleship training to equip Christian believers to live like Jesus did, we neglect the other part of Jesus' example: searching for, rescuing and winning the lost, teaching them about God's love, and encouraging them to return home to God for a fresh start (Lk 15:1–32).

The most important biblical directive (or path) for our life and ministry could be found in the Great Commission (Mt 28:19–20), which is *disciple making*, people making disciples who make disciples. The solution is for church leaders and the congregation to lead a balanced biblical life: evangelism and discipleship. Otherwise, we can end up with a distorted ecclesiology when we need a strong Christology (Spader, 2012, p. 145).

Storytelling the Disciple Making Path has explored how Jesus' disciple making process can be applied to the present culture. This Bible study material is about understanding cultural shifts that influence us all, much like a coastal water tide is influenced by the phases of the moon. In this cultural tidal movement, we understand the disciple making path is influenced by *three* directional moves that must take place, if you or your church wants to become a disciple making community for Jesus. These *three* directional moves along the disciple making path are easy to remember.

1. Move from **disconnecting to connecting** (Mt 13:3–24).
     share to win, then connect

2. Move from **informing to preparing** (Mt 10; Lk 10; Eph 4:11–16).
     build to move

3. Move from **accumulating to sending** (Mk 6:7; Lk 10:1–3).
     train to send

These directional movements generate a committed group of people who move others to grow from spiritual death to spiritual life as followers of Jesus, to spiritual maturity, to make disciples, who go on making other disciples, who walk along through the *increasing* features of the disciple making path.

- **Increasing** oneself, a follower of Christ (Jn 17:4, 18; Mt 28:19–20; Acts 14:21).
- Disciples who make other disciples, helping people to trust and follow Jesus, and grow towards spiritual maturity.
- **Increasing** spiritually mature disciples for Christ (Heb 5:11–6:2; Col 1:28).
- Spiritually mature disciples love and care for spiritual infants and spiritual children.
- **Increasing** volunteers for service (Acts 2:45; 6:1–6).
- Church leaders train and teach disciples to serve or become involved in a church activity.
- **Increasing** seed sowers and harvest workers (Lk 10:2; Mt 9:38).
- Church leaders train and teach disciples (in small groups), to move along the disciple making path. Small group leaders train and teach disciples (in small groups), for Storytelling Jesus' Story.
- **Increasing** leaders and one's ministry (Jn 21:15–17).
- Leaders making leaders, training spiritual mature disciples towards a future ministry of shepherd leadership.
  We also believe *increasing* leaders can be seen with Jesus and his brothers James and Jude (Acts 1:14; 15:13; 1 Cor 15:7; Gal 1:18–19; Jms 1:1; Jud 1:1), Ananias and Paul (Acts 9:1–31), and with Paul and Timothy (Acts 17:14–15).

How can we achieve the *increasing* features along Jesus' disciple making path? We have found the answer to that question is using the Storytelling Jesus' Story method.

Storytelling Jesus' Story

This Bible study material applies the features of the *increasing* disciple making path through 9 studies of storytelling and discussion. We believe the only primary pursuit in disciple making is speaking God's Word. One way of doing this is *Storytelling Jesus' Story*. It is a simple way for people to re-tell or speak a small portion of one of Jesus' stories, and they can learn it in the relational environment of a small group or growth group.

To be a storyteller of Jesus' story we need to be like a translator. Our aim is to put the story in a new form, to speak the language of the hearer. We want to communicate Jesus' stories in a more understandable form but retain the original concepts, as a translator would do from one language to another. We are translating the story told to a Greco-Roman, first century Palestine audience, to the present day audience. Our desire is to speak a fresh and clear word to the modern context today, without seriously changing the content of the story (Erickson, 1985, p. 113). More about stories and storytelling Jesus' story are found at the end of Study 4 and throughout Study's 8 to 16.

Disciple Making Inspiration and Approach

There is a real need to move our focus onto biblical disciple making in our relational or social networks. Our purpose has never ever been solely to teach the Bible, or evangelism, or discipleship. It has always been about *disciple making*. This includes Biblical instruction (proclaiming God's Word), evangelism (search, rescue and win the lost) and discipleship (equipping to live like Jesus did). Therefore, our starting point is the Great Commission (Mt 28:19–20) and our calling is to be disciples who make other disciples, in an eternal relationship with Jesus (Mt 28:20b; Lk 24:49; Jn 20:31).

When our eternal relationship with Jesus is right, all other real relationships fall into place. Real relationships involve doing life with people and journeying together in everyday relational environments such as workplaces, family and social networks. The purpose is to introduce people to Jesus with the invitation to *"come and see"* (Jn 1:39, 46), to trust that he is the one who speaks on God's behalf (Lk 4:14–22) and to answer Jesus' call to *"come follow me"* (Mt 4:19). Remember, it is Jesus who converts them, not us. We simply introduce them to Jesus and leave it up to Jesus. Yet we can still show them God's love, by encouraging them to turn back to God (which is repentance) and find forgiveness of sins (Lk 24:47), to have a new and fresh start, to become devoted to God and his purpose for our lives. This connects God's story to their story for a better eternal ending to their life.

The greatest disciple maker in history was Jesus. The early Christians had no doubt about the importance of Jesus' teachings and their responsibility to teach them to new converts (Acts 2:42–46). Therefore, disciple making is our vision, encouragement, and inspiration.

Commitment to the Commission

All church leaders and ministries need to be committed to Jesus' Great Commission. That is, every growth group, Bible study group, Sunday school class, youth group, men's breakfast, ladies' night, seniors' group, needs to be fully committed to *"making disciples"* (Mt 28:19). All church ministry teams need some sort of disciple making devotional, or prayer focus. That includes pastors, elders, deacons, ministry leaders, small group leaders, youth leaders, and the church office administration team. Devotions and prayers should focus on topics such as disciples who make disciples growing towards spiritual maturity, and journeying through life together with others in every day relational environments (Powers, 2010, p. 261).

Whatever your role in the church, whatever your level of learning, if you have been a Christian for 30 years or 30 days, God is going to do some remarkable things with you. Making disciples (helping people to believe and follow Jesus) is a God-given directive to the church, and you are an integral part of your local church.

Loyal disciples attract people because of the change they see in their Christ-like lives.

The method outlined in this guide, *Storytelling the Disciple Making Path*, encourages, inspires, and empowers Christians to be more like Christ and intentionally develop relationships with non-believers, spiritually young believers, and mature peer-to-peer followers of Jesus.

Disciple Making Path

Jesus performed relational disciple making in the culture of his day (the first century Greco-Roman world), leaving us a path for disciple making in our modern context today. Jesus spent over half of his ministry life (approx. 18 months) until appointing the Twelve. Then he sent out the *twelve* (Mt 10:1–4), and later the *seventy-two* (Lk 10:1–24), to make disciples who make disciples. Then *one hundred and twenty* (Acts 1:15) are sent out into Jerusalem, Judea, and Samaria, and to the ends of the earth (Acts 1:8). These disciples grew to maturity, as spiritual parents, who cared for spiritual infants and child believers (2 Cor 6:18; 1 Thess 2:6–12), moving them towards spiritual maturity (Eph 4:12–13) (Spader, 2012, p. 52). Along the increasing features of the disciple making path (increasing workers for the harvest and workers for service). As they appointed shepherd leaders (increasing leaders and one's ministry). As God sent Jesus, so Jesus is sending you (Jn 20:21) as a disciple who makes other disciples (Mt 28:19–20), to go and bear good fruit (Jn 15:16). The simplicity of Jesus' disciple making path is so incredible that we might wonder how we failed to see it before.

Biblical References

- Go and make disciples of all nations… teaching them to obey everything I have commanded you. And surely, I am with you always, to the very end of the age (Mt 28:19–20).
- I have set you an example that you should do as I have done for you (Jn 13:15).
- I have brought you glory on earth by finishing the work you gave me to do (Jn 17:4).
- As you sent me into the world, I have sent them into the world (Jn 17:18).
- Jesus said, "Peace be with you! As the Father has sent me, I am sending you" (Jn 20:21).
- Jesus said, "If you hold to my teaching, you are really my disciples. Then you will know the truth, and the truth will set you free" (Jn 8:31–32).
- Whoever believes in me will do the works I have been doing, and they will do even greater things than these, because I am going to the Father (Jn 14:12).
- His intent was that now, through the church, the manifold wisdom of God should be made known to the rulers and authorities in the heavenly realms, according to his eternal purpose that he accomplished in Christ Jesus our Lord (Ep 3:10–11).

MOVE TOWARD SPIRITUAL MATURITY

THIS DIRECTION HELPS US TO MOVE ALONG JESUS' disciple making path from spiritual immaturity as a vulnerable infant disciple to becoming a responsible spiritual mentor, carer, or parent.

What is a Disciple?

The word, "*disciple*" is the New Testament Greek word, *mathetes*, which means, "*a learner*" (Rayburn, p. 216). But more, an *active learner*, actively learning to live like their teacher (Marshall & Payne, p. 64). A disciple can also refer to a student of a teacher. The Pharisees had disciples (Lk 5:33) and so did John the Baptist (Jn 1:35; Lk 7:18). A disciple follows a teacher and is *actively learning* to live like their teacher. This seems to be hard wired into all humanity because, everyone follows something or someone and learns to become like that person. John Calvin states it well (1960, p. 108), "We are a perpetual factory of idols". However, Jesus said, "*No one can serve two masters*" (Mt 6:24).

Every person on this earth has a choice (by default) of two options. The first option is to follow, learn the ways of this world and its negative voices, and become a disciple of "*the evil one*" (2 Cor 4:4; 1 Jn 3:8, 10; 2 Pt 2:2–3), and the spiritual forces of this world (Col 2:8, 20), that drive or enslave people throughout their life. The evil one could be seen as the Inner Critic. The Inner Critic is a psychological term, for the one who keeps telling us, "You are stupid, dumb, immature, fat, thin, ugly, horrible." Or the one who wakes us up at 5.00am and reminds us of a bad experience we went through, in the past. These negative words throughout one's life have been changing the neural pathways in our brain, which changes our behavior, which drives one or two of the following (anger, anxiety, feeling down, worry or fear), throughout our lives. And the Inner Critic is laughing in the background (Thompson, 2019).

The second option is to choose to be a disciple of Jesus Christ, to be built up in him, strengthened in faith (Col 2:6), becoming like Christ (1 Jn 2:6; 1 Cor 11:1), by actively learning to live like him, which shrinks and starves the evil one and those negative voices.

Who Then is a Disciple of Jesus?

Read Matthew 4:17–22; 2 Corinthians 3:1618– and 2 Corinthians 5:15–20. These passages give us a clear model for understanding a real disciple of Jesus. Spend a few minutes going over these three passages to identify a disciple of Jesus.

(See Leaders' Notes 1).

Q: A Disciple of Jesus is a Person who?

Has	(Mt 4:17)
Has	(2 Cor 3:16)
Has	(2 Cor 3:17)
No longer lives for	(2 Cor 5:15)
Is not	(2 Cor 5:16)
Is a	(2 Cor 5:17)
Is	to Christ (2 Cor 5:18-20)
Has	(2 Cor 5:19)
Has been given the	of reconciliation (2 Cor 5:19)
Is an	for Christ (2 Cor 5:20)

Most importantly a disciple of Jesus is a person who follows Jesus. Matthew 4:19 reads, *"Come follow me* [and] *I will teach you how to catch people."* Let us unpack this verse to discover how a disciple is related to the *contemplation*, *central focus*, and the *practical hands on*.

Contemplation

A disciple starts to contemplate as the light of Jesus illuminates our thinking, and we move from being disconnected to being connected as we first spend time with him and his Word and in prayer. In Jesus' words, *"Come follow me"* is a beautiful invitation to accept who Jesus is and the reality of his integrity as our Lord and redeemer. He is the one who is 100% God and 100% human, simultaneously (Jn 1:1, 14, 41). And, he is not only the *"way"* to heaven, but he is also the *reality and the means of all "truth," that leads to eternal "life"* (Jn 14:6).

As previously stated, the word, *"disciple"* means a follower who *actively learns* from a teacher. To follow Jesus is to *actively learn* from his teaching, to live like he did. A follower of Jesus understands who Jesus is. He is the Boss of our lives. He leads us from the front, and we follow behind him. John 12:26 explains this process: *"Whoever serves me must follow me; and where I am, my servant also will be."* As we study Jesus' biographies (the Gospels), we actively learn to live a whole new life for Jesus. When we follow Jesus, we become a *mathetes*, a disciple, a follower, an active learner.

Central Focus

Transformation is the central focus of a disciple. *"I will teach you"* (Mt 4:19) is what Jesus does to his disciples (followers who actively learn). Jesus shapes and models our hearts to become more like him. A disciple of Jesus is changed by Jesus. We are conformed into the image of Christ (Rom 8:29), as we actively learn to live like he did.

Jesus transforms how we see the world, what we value and consider important. This happens as we allow God's Spirit to change our inner being (Rom 12:2; 2 Cor 3:18). Therefore, we are changed to be actively hands on people.

Practical Hands on

Jesus states, a disciple will be taught *"how to catch people"* (Mt 4:19). In other words, a disciple will be actively hands on, *making disciples who make disciples*. A disciple of Jesus is rescued and freed for a purpose and that purpose is to join Jesus on his disciple making path to connect and reach a lost and hurting world (Lk 19:10). Catching people is a call to action as we use our abilities, gifts, talents, and whatever God has placed in our hands to serve Jesus in disciple making, which God has *"prepared in advance for us to do"* (Eph 2:10).

Consequently, we see from Matthew 4:19 that a disciple of Jesus is a person who **follows and learns from Jesus, being changed by Jesus**, and **joins Jesus on his disciple making path**.

Importantly, a disciple of Jesus lives out a lifestyle of "sentness,"[1] by being a disciple who makes other disciples or increasing oneself: *"as you sent me into the world, I have sent them into the world"* (Jn 17:18). But is there more to this? Yes, it is about disciples who make other disciples who move toward spiritual maturity. Our goal is to present people as spiritually mature in Christ (1 Cor 14:20; Col 1:28; Heb 5:14; Jms 1:4). When this is our goal, it changes everything.

If we want to make disciples, then where do we start? How can we start growing spiritual mature people for Jesus? Let us look at the stages of spiritual growth.

---

1 All through the Gospel of John is the word, "sent" from that word, we get the expression, "sentness" (North, 2015).

Five Stages of Spiritual Growth

As a follower of Jesus, we walk along the disciple making path, we also need to recognise there are stages or movements towards spiritual growth. It is important to identify the five spiritual stages of growth of a disciple, understand the basic characteristics and needs of each stage, and recognise key statements that people say in each stage (Putman & Harrington, 2013, p. 59). This will help the disciple develop and move forward to spiritual maturity.

Bible Reading

Read Ephesians 2:1–2, 5; 1 Peter 2:2; 1 John 2:12–14 and 1 Thessalonians 2:7, 11 and pray that God will speak to you through his Word. Go over these nine verses as a group and answer the following five questions.

Q: What spiritual growth stages do the below verses indicate?

Ephesians 2:1–2, 5.

Note: From conversion, a disciple has their *identity* in Christ (1 Jn 3:1). God made them alive with Christ (Col 2:13). They live a new life (Rom 6:4), through spiritual re-birth, being born of God (1 Jn 5:1), which implies having an ongoing, personal relationship with God through Jesus Christ. God gives us a new identity in Christ, and it is as saved disciples that we grow into our new identity.

1 Peter 2:2.
1 John 2:12a.

In the below passages, your Bible may use masculine terms, therefore use neutral terms that are neither masculine nor feminine.[2]

---

2 The word, "young men" is the (Gr neaniskoi) which is translated "young people," which applies to women as well (Johnson, 1993, p. 50).

1 John 2:13b, 14b.[3]

Again, your Bible may use a masculine term, so use a neutral one, that is both male and female.[4]

1 John 2:13a, 14a, 1 Thessalonians 2:7, 11.

From these passages, a disciple has made a move from being **spiritually dead**,[5] to a spiritual infant by being spiritually re-born by God at the point of conversion. A new believer finds repentance and forgiveness and dies to the network of lies that their lives were constructed on. John uses imagery of a new birth: *"reborn …not [by] a physical birth … but a birth that comes from God"* (Jn 1:13 NLT); *born of the Spirit* (Jn 3:8); *born of God* (1 Jn 2:29; 3:8, 9; 5:1). Peter states they are *"like newborn babies, [who] crave pure spiritual milk, so that by it* [they] *may grow up in* [their] *salvation"* (1 Pt 2:2). Then a disciple moves from being a **spiritual infant** to a **spiritual child** to a **spiritual young adult** to a **mature spiritual parent.** The Bold emphases is for the answers for the previous five questions.

Why are these five growth stages of spiritual maturity important to know? Well, let us have a look at them.

Importance of the Five Stages of Spiritual Maturity

Too many Christians stay in the infant or child level for years, never maturing (Heb 5:12–6:1a). They have no understanding about purposefully building relationships with non-Christians who are spiritually dead, who are lost and unengaged, like they

---

3 There are three different spiritual levels, out of the five, in 1 John 2:12-14, (children, young people and parents), cited from Matthews, 2017.

4 The word, "father/s" refers to mature believers, both male and female (Akin, 2014, p. 37), which we would call "parents".

5 The spiritually dead (not saved) are enslaved in their thinking to the Inner Critic and are opposed to learning from Jesus' teaching. People that are "dead in your sins" (Col 2:13). Sin is basically, using God's resources (relationships, money, environment etc.), but living at a distance from Him, as seen in the story of the lost son, in Luke 15:11-32. The good news is that through Jesus and God's love they can turn back to God, becoming spiritually reborn, made alive again.

once were. This is done by sharing life together and having general conversations. Where? In relational and social environments. This leads to spiritual conversations and provides an invitation to *"come and see"* (John 1:39), to check out the facts and the truth about who Jesus is. It is followed by an invitation to follow Jesus (Jn 1:40, 43; Mt 4:19, 9:19; Lk 5:11), turning back to God as Jesus proclaimed, *"repent and believe"* (Mt 4:17; Jn 3:36), or as Paul puts it, turn to the Lord (2 Cor 3:16). Actively learning to live like Christ has done when we win spiritually dead people for Jesus. That is, to engage their minds, hearts and then their hands for Christ, making the transformation from being *lost* and *dead*, to being *rescued* and *alive again* (Lk 15:32), alive for Christ (2 Cor 5:15) and actively learning to live like Christ.

Many spiritual young adults and mature believers don't really understand the need to be parents (1 Thess 2:11). Spiritual infants and children need spiritual older siblings and mature parents to help them connect with other believers and disciples. For example, having a coffee, one-on-one conversations after church or participating in a Bible study small group, or volunteering in a church activity. Let our *"people learn to devote themselves to good works, in order to meet urgent needs, so that they may not be unproductive"* (Titus 3:14 NRSV). It is important to be connected to biblical, relational environments.

Biblical, relational environments are small groups (also called growth groups or fellowship groups), whether mid-week or on the weekend for support, encouragement, fellowship, for following and actively learning from Jesus' teachings (Heb 10:25; Col 3:16; 2 Tim 3:16–17). And then there is the corporate church worship service for community connection, worship, growth, prayer, service and social interaction. The word, "Church" is first mentioned in Acts 11:20-21, yet the Israelites had been corporately gathering for centuries (Deut 31:12; Ps 133:1; Ex 20:8-11).

Importantly, the disciple making path is the direction for one's life and mission, and it is the same for the church today (Jn 17:18), *"As you sent me into the world, I have sent them into the world"*. Disciples who make disciples who MOVE towards spiritual maturity (1 Cor 14:20; Col 1:28; Heb 5:14; Jms 1:4), through the five stages of spiritual growth, as they walk along the following three directional MOVES, which are very easy to remember.

1. Move from **disconnecting to connecting** (Mt 13:3–24).
    share to win, then connect

2. Move from **informing to preparing** (Mt 10; Lk 10; Eph 4:11–16).
    build to move

3. Move from **accumulating to sending** (Mk 6:7; Lk 10:1–3).
    train to send

When a spiritual infant moves beyond the spiritual milk of righteousness (Heb 5:13), into the elementary teachings about Christ they become a spiritual child who is no longer tossed around by every false teaching (Eph 4:14). A spiritual child has discovered their spiritual gifts, is grounded in the teachings of repentance, faith in God, baptism, laying on of hands, the resurrection, eternal judgment, the indwelling of the Holy Spirit, the goodness of God's Word, the powers of the coming age, confidence in their salvation and the work of disciples who make other disciples (Heb 6:1–10). A spiritual child moves towards spiritual maturity (Eph 4:15). There is no place for mental laziness or being slow to learn (Heb 5:11, 6:12).

The Key is: When a spiritual child starts to make disciple who make disciples, they become a spiritual young adult very quickly (Eph 4:14–16). These disciples have been nourished by spiritual food (Heb 5:14), and now they need spiritual exercise to keep growing.

Application – For Now and in the Future

Spend 5 minutes in preparation for the application and complete the following questions.

(See Leaders' Notes 2)

Q: Write down what makes you a real disciple. Do you follow Jesus, do you know what your spiritual gifts are, and are you being changed by Jesus, to make disciples? Or is there something missing?

____

____

____

____

Q: How many years have you been a Christian? Circle your answer.

1-5 years
6-10 years
11-15 year
16-20 years
21-29 years
30 years and over

Q: What stage of spiritual maturity do you have? Think it through. Be honest! Circle your answer. Afterwards, share this with the group.

Spiritually Dead / Infant / Child / Young Adult / Mature Parent

Prayer

We pray that God will help us move from being a spiritual infant to a spiritually mature parent. Give us an opportunity to share life by purposefully building relationships with non-Christians, in relational environments, to win them for you Jesus. Help us Lord, to look after new believers, warning them about destructive cults and their deceitful schemes and from the discouragement of this world and its prince. Also, help them to connect into small groups, church worship services and church ministry (biblical, relational environments).

Note: The weekend corporate worship could be on Saturday evening or Sunday morning or evening.

Preparation for the Next Study

Go over the spiritual growth stages and why they are important. Familiarize yourself by memorizing the three directional MOVES, the increasing features in the disciple making path and read Study 2.

MOVE FROM DISCONNECTING TO CONNECTING (PART 1)

THIS DIRECTION HELPS US TO MOVE OUR THINKING from being disconnected to people, to making disciples. To win spiritually dead people for Jesus, we should understand the Five Plus Five, and the post-Christian society that we inhabit.

Five Plus Five

A non-Christian must get to know five good Christian believers and have heard the gospel message more than five times before they can understand and believe it (Spader, 2012, p. 39).

It is essential that all disciples of Christ purposefully build relationships with non-Christians, people who are spiritually dead, as we once were (Eph 2:1–2), by being salt and light to the world (Mt 5:13–16), using a model that can be described as prayer, care and share (North, 2015). Remembering that Jesus is with us (Mt 28:20), we share life together (1 Thess 2:8) through deeds and words, praying for people by name, caring for their heart-felt needs and doing acts of kindness and by relating to them in conversation (Mt 9:35). This happens best in social environments, especially in environments that lead to sharing spiritual conversations with people who are open and eventually sharing an invitation to hear the gospel message *"come and see"* (Jn 1:39), to check out the facts about who Jesus is. The major fact would be, Jesus' humanity and deity, the one who is fully God and fully human, at the same time (Jn 1:1, 14, 41).

Another fact would be, why are his teachings so inground into today's Western society? Jesus' teachings that are accepted today are – The equality of all people, care for the poor and marginalized, dignity of women and children, education and health care for everyone, forgiveness, democracy, being generous and being wise with money, all have their beginnings in Jesus' teachings (Faase, 2016, p. 1).

Then an invitation to turn back to God and believe (Mt 4:17; Jn 3:36), and follow Jesus (Jn 1:43), for a whole new fresh start in life.

But we need to understand the intellectual environment that could determine how our conversations are shaped.

The Post-Christian Shift

Before World War 2 (WW2) the Western world used Scripture as their *Reference Point*. They believed that a Supreme Being had revealed to them his blueprint on how humanity was to operate purposefully, functionally, and productively in the world he lovely created. The evidence of Scripture with its *Reference Point* can be also seen through archaeology, prophecy and the experience of millions and millions of eyewitnesses, since the dawn of time. These people have travelled its pathway and have interconnected its storyline into their own.

At that time, every law in the Western world was based on the Word of God, the Bible, and it gave us stability and structure to our lives (Zimmermann, 2024, pp. 1-2). The English *Magna Carta* (1215 A.D.), the American *Declaration of Independence* (1776 A.D.), and the Australian *Rule of Law* (1900 A.D.), are all grounded on the ancient reliable manuscripts of the 66 books in the Bible (Holdsworth, pp. 1-4). The Bible was the *Reference Point* for what we BELIEVED in, LIVED, FOUGHT and DIED for.

However, after WW2 there was a huge shift away from the biblical reference point. The shift was so huge that it created its own pathway. It was like they moved the whole path to the left, leaving us as Christians on the right side, as fanatical toxic haters.

Yet we haven't changed, because our *Reference Point* is still on Scripture and its beautiful storyline. So, what happened for this shift to take place and what is now their reference point?

To combat against the possible influences of Communism, the Western culture shifted towards Democracy! The word, "Democracy" comes from the Greek word, "*demoskratia*" meaning, "*the people have the power to rule*" (Macquarie, p. 329). Therefore, the reference point for democracy is "*what matters is what the people think*." And with this, humanity has been aimlessly drifting along ever since (Westlake, 2024).

Today, the cultural shift goes far beyond moving from modernism to postmodernism (Audi, 1995, p. 634), from truth as science proves everything, to truth is experiential and personal (there is no absolute truth). The average unchurched person is not searching for absolute truth. Rather, they are looking for real truth that resounds with their life experiences. They want to know what is true to life, in their life. They are looking for faith, faith that is lived out and spiritual experiences that are real and genuine (Richardson, 2000, pp. 45–46). Well, maybe the truth about Jesus and the biblical Reference Point can set them free. But what if they do not know anything at all about God, Jesus, and the Bible.

The average unchurched person has become a non-believer because they do not know why they even need to believe in God, let alone follow Jesus. Their need is to understand Christianity as truth because everything we believe to be true (e.g., freedom, identity, meaning, hope, satisfaction, and morality) are ludicrous without the God of the Bible also being true. "We all cannot exist without a transcendent God who made us, loves us and saves us" (Chan, 2020, p. 130).

Nevertheless, we want you to know that our Reference Point is Scripture, and we want to walk along its trustworthy and reliable pathway, as millions of other people have journeyed along, since the commencement of time.

As a group answer the following four questions.

Q: What do you think about "Five plus Five"?

____

____

____

Q: Have you seen these post-Christian shifts in your lifetime?

____

____

____

Q: Will You, from this point on, try to better understand today's culture, to win the lost for Jesus.

Yes / No

The early apostles proclaimed the gospel and won disciples (Acts 14:21). As the people we are sharing with respond to and follow Jesus (Mt 4:19), they are spiritually re-born. They experience a move from being spiritually dead, to becoming a spiritual infant. John uses imagery of a new birth: *"reborn ...not [by] a physical birth ... but a birth that comes from God"* (Jn 1:13 NLT). Elsewhere, it is described as being reborn, *"like newborn babies"* who need *"pure spiritual milk"* so they *"may grow up in their salvation"* (1 Pt 2:2).

A new believer can be described as a *spiritual infant*; someone who has put their trust in Jesus and become a disciple of Jesus. They follow Jesus, are changed by Jesus, and are committed to his mission, by reaching out into the community, making disciples who make other disciples (Mt 28:19–20), who move towards spiritual maturity (Col 1:28). Most church mission statements, or church values reflect this process in words such as "reach out."

The Author's Mission Statement: Storytelling the disciple making path, using the *Reference Point* of Scripture, through small groups, serving, teaching, and speaking, to feed others to do the same.

Q: What is your mission statement? Please write it down.

Then Connect

We help new disciples connect with other disciples in relational environments. For example, having a coffee one-on-one, being in a small group, or being involved in a church service, ministry or activity. These environments should concentrate on teaching people to obey Jesus' teachings (Mt 28:20), by building disciple relationships as he did. It is important to connect new disciples into a biblical relational environment for fellowship which supports people as they move towards spiritual maturity and practice disciple-making (Putman & Harrington, 2013, pp. 158–159).

Bible Reading

(See Leaders' Notes 3)

Read Matthew 13:3–23. Pray that God will speak to you through his word. After, spend ten minutes going over the passage and answering the following questions. Afterwards, share your answers with the group.

Q: What do you notice for the first time? What stood out to you?

Q: As you think about this passage, what do you wonder about? What questions does it raise?

Q: What might this passage reveal to us about Jesus, his work and his plans?

Application – for Now and in the Future

Spend 5 minutes in preparation for the application. Afterwards, share your answers with the group.

Q. At this point in time, do you think you are in the first directional move (Share to Win / Then Connect)?

Think it through and be honest. Circle your answer.

Yes or No.

If NO, how are you going to move to Share to Win / Then Connect?

If YES, how are you going to move to the next stage?

Alternatively, in one sentence, write down one aspect of what you learnt from this passage.

Prayer

We pray that God will give us an opportunity to share life by purposefully building relationships with non-Christians, in relational environments to introduce them to Jesus, by persuading them about God's love, to turn back to God for a fresh start in life. Help us, Lord, to sow into the good soil of open doors for the gospel message and help us to parent new believers and connect them into small groups for fellowship and into the corporate church service for biblical worship.

Preparation for the Next Study

Go over and familiarize yourself with Five Plus Five, the Post-Christian Shift, and read Study 3.

MOVE FROM DISCONNECTING TO CONNECTING (PART 2)

THIS DIRECTION REMINDS US TO MOVE OUR THINKING from being disconnected to people, to making disciples. To win spiritually dead people for Jesus, we should understand that it's not all about evangelism.

Disciple Making, not Evangelism

Stan May (2007, p. 342) states, "Evangelism means to make disciples." But it is not, because spending lots of time on evangelism is like spending lots of time on a wedding day but not on the marriage. We are in danger of spending so much time winning people for Christ that we overlook disciple making. A marriage is not a onetime decision, it is a daily decision to love someone and work through different situations. It is incorrect to think of a onetime confession for Christ as being the most important thing, and not understanding that it is a daily relationship of following Christ that matters. We were never called to evangelise, we were called to be disciple makers, a process which includes but is not limited to evangelism (Putman, 2015).

Turning Evangelism and Discipleship Upside Down

So, we realise that it is all about disciple making. However, evangelising first and then discipling afterwards, does not always work, all that well. It seems that these two processes should be reversed. Why not disciple people first, where they are at, by building relationships? (Matthews, 2009). This involves having general conversations that lead to spiritual conversations about Jesus' teaching. His teaching could include, the equality of all humanity, forgiveness, servant leadership, care for the poor and marginalised, the dignity of women and children, the importance of education and health care, to name just a few. This later leads to an invitation to hear the gospel message, *"come and see"* (Jn 1:39), checking out the facts about who Jesus is. Then, they can respond to following Jesus (Jn 1:43), or as the Apostle Paul puts it, turn to the Lord (2 Cor 3:16) and live for Christ (2 Cor 5:15), which is the evangelism part.

You see, through disciple making, the whole idea of sharing our faith is turned upside down; not for bad, but for *good*. This should not surprise us, because Jesus did that two thousand years ago and he is still doing it today; turning people and situations around, for *good*.

Spiritual Maturity

Now that we know how integral disciple making is and what it looks like when coupled with evangelism and discipleship, let us see how we can help people move forward. Identifying the spiritual stages people are in, can sound challenging. However, promoting this step is a beneficial move in the progress of a disciple. It is an assessment of spiritual maturity, designed to help people move forward in their spiritual walk. Remember, our goal is to present everyone as mature in Christ (Col 1:28). We want to create an increasing movement of mature disciple makers who can make disciples. This responsibility rests on the shoulders of three key persons; the disciple maker, the person being discipled and God (Faase, 2016, p. 1).

Recap: In study 1, we identified the five spiritual growth stages of a disciple, but let's also look at their basic characteristics and needs.

Spiritually Dead

Those who are dead in their sins (Col 2:13; Eph 2:1–3), who are potential disciples and need to be saved by Christ, to be re-born or made alive with Christ (Eph 2:5), becoming a follower of Christ, who are being changed by Christ, who are committed to his disciple making mission (Matt 4:19; 28:19).

For those who accept Jesus, we are then *"made… alive in Christ"* (Col 2:13), through spiritual re-birth, being *"born of God"* (1 John 3:9; 5:18), *"born of the Spirit"* (Jn 3:8), becoming children of God.

"Yet to all who did receive him, to those who believed in his name, he gave the right to become children of God - children born not of natural descent, nor of human decision or a husband's will, but born of God" (Jn 1:12–13).

Being made alive in Christ means that you now have an ongoing, personal relationship with God through Jesus Christ, because you have confessed your sins to God and that you believe that you will live with God for eternity exclusively, because of the grace extended to you through that relationship with Jesus.

Infant

Newborn babies who crave pure spiritual milk, so they can grow in their salvation (1 Pt 2:2–3). A spiritual infant is vulnerable and in need of a spiritual parent or a spiritual big brother or big sister to help and guide them, as any newborn does.

Spiritual Child

Someone young in their faith, *"little children"* (*1* Jn 2:12 NRSV), who need the basic foundational teaching about Christ (Heb 6:1,2), who need to start making disciples who make disciples (Mt 28:19–20), (even if it is one-step-at-a-time), which would help them move quickly into being a spiritual young adult.

Spiritual Young Adult

A spiritual young person, who has overcome the evil one, who is strong, because God's Word remains in them (1 Jn 2:13–14). A spiritual young person is no longer a child tossed around by every wind of deception, scam, or deceitful teaching. But are grownups who speak and live the truth in love about Jesus, who have grown into the likeness and person of Christ (Eph 4:14–15). They need to start looking after spiritual infants and spiritual children, like a big brother or big sister.

Spiritual Parent or Mentor

God is the one who gives spiritual birth to people, so we are not parents in this way. Yet it is God's plan for spiritual parents to help guide spiritual newborns and children toward spiritual maturity (1 Thess 2:7–8, 11–12). Maybe the word, "mentor" might be a better term. Someone who helps, guides and encourages spiritual infants and children in their walk with Jesus. Or may be a "coach" someone who teaches and trains spiritual infants and children to work together, like in a team, making disciples together for Christ. Whatever term is used, a spiritual mature believer is a person who knows the difference between good and evil (Heb 5:14), who is very strong in their faith, who has moved towards perfection (Heb 6:1). Here the word *"perfection"* means, spiritual maturity (Putman & Harrington, 2013, p. 74).

Reflection

To help understand the basic characteristics and needs of each spiritual stage, spend a few minutes answering the following question.

Q: What do you think would be the basic needs of each spiritual stage?

(See Leaders' Notes 4)

Spiritually Dead

Their needs are…

Spiritual Infant

Their needs are…

Spiritual Child

Their needs are…

Spiritual Young Adult

Their needs are…

Spiritual Mature Parent

Their needs are…

What People Say in Each Stage and Helping Them to Move Forward

Jesus taught that when people speak, their words will reveal their spiritual stage. *"A good person brings good things out of the good stored up in his heart, and an evil person brings evil things out of the evil stored up in his heart. For the mouth speaks what the heart is full of"* (Lk 6:45).

Spiritually Dead People Might Say:

- I don't believe there really is a God. The Bible is just a load of rubbish full of mistakes (Shelton, p. 839).
- Prayer! What is that going to do? There are many paths that lead to some sort of a deity.
- Christians are unloving, judgmental, critical people, who speak hate.
- I have lots of money, therefore I don't need God.
- All my life, I've been a good person, so when I die, I deserve to go to heaven.
- I am a spiritual person, but I don't connect with any particular religion.
- There is no right or wrong. If something is right for you, it might not be right for me, and vice versa.

Helping a Spiritually Dead Person Move Forward:

- They need your prayers to open their eyes and ears, as well as to soften their hearts. If you need a reminder, pray for the harvest at 10.02 a.m. each day, which is linked to Luke 10:2 (Munn, 2016).
- Care and share by connecting them into honest friendships and relationships with believers. Introduce your Christian friends to your non-Christian friends in relational environments.

- Introduce them to Jesus and help them to see the life of the gospel lived out through you. Help them to answer their questions about the Bible, God, life, heaven and Christianity (Putman & Harrington, 2013, p. 61).
- Tell them one of Jesus' stories then ask: "Why do you think Jesus did that".

Spiritual Infant Might Say:

- I need to go to church more often. I've never heard anything like that before. Where is that in the Bible?
- I need to pray, read and study the Bible on a regular basis? Wow! I didn't know the Bible said that (Putman & Harrington, 2013, p. 61).
- What's tithing? How much? Ten percent! Do I have to?
- I am an outdoor person, and that is how I connect with God. Walking in the bushland is my church.
- You know, I can be a Christian and not go to church. It's all about Jesus and me.
- I feel like I'm an infant and I need someone to care for me.
- I thought Jesus would take care of all our problems. On the way to church my wife and I got into a big fight. I walked into the church door with steam coming out of my ears. What a great way to start worshiping God.

Helping a Spiritual Infant Move Forward:

- They need a mature spiritual parent to care and feed them. They need protection and guidance from being led astray. Warn them about false cults such as Mormons and Jehovah witnesses, or so-called Christian television programs that causes disciples to believe in promises that the Bible doesn't make.
- They need the truth of the Christian faith taught to them, so they can develop new habits and patterns for living as a follower of Christ (Putman & Harrington, 2013, p. 63).

- If they don't want to go to church, they need to be encouraged to go to a to a regular home group.

Spiritual Children Might Say:

- I don't know if this church is meeting my needs anymore. Maybe I should go to a different church.
- Don't divide our small group into two groups. We won't get to be with our friends.
- Who are all these new people coming into our church? The church is getting too big.
- I think I can be a Christian and not go to church.
- I have heard about faith deconstruction. I think I don't want to be a Christian anymore.
- Why do we have to learn new songs? I like the old hymns better.
- I didn't like the old hymns. They should play more contemporary music.
- No one ever says hello to me at church. No one ever calls me to see how I'm doing. No one spends time with me. The pastor doesn't care about me, and today he didn't even say hello.
- My small group is not taking care of my needs like they should.
- I wasn't fed at all by that sermon or the Bible study today.
- Why don't they have a ministry to singles at this church? This church must not care about singles.
- Christians shouldn't listen to hip-hop or rock. That kind of music is just unchristian.
- I was helping in children's ministry, but they didn't appreciate what I was doing, so I quit (Putman & Harrington, 2013, p. 64).

Helping Spiritual Children Move Forward:

- They need teaching about who they are in Christ, how to have close friendships with other believers, and what to expect and not expect from Christians.
- They need to learn to trust God, doing what God's Word says rather than what their feelings tell them to do.
- They need a spiritual mentor to pray with regularly, to help them focus outwardly.
- They need to know what it means to have a servant heart, rather than being self-centred (Putman & Harrington, 2013, p. 66).
- They need to be encouraged to persevere. Show them the short YouTube video, *"The Persistent Widow"* (Matthews, 2022).
- They need to be taught about the Inner Critic who whispers in their ear, "You're stupid, dumb, fat, thin, ugly, you don't need to go to church, and chuck your faith in."
- They need to be shown how to shrink and starve the Inner Critic with true word statements, because the truth will set you free (Jn 8:32). See the handout in Study 15.

Spiritual Young Adults Might Say:

- In my devotion, I came across something I have a question about.
- I would like to stop being a Christian, but I know I'll be worse off.
- I really want to go on a mission trip this year. I know I'm ready for it. I know God has big plans for my life.
- I love that I am the small group apprentice. Our small group leader is helping prepare me for a future role as a small group leader.
- I just love being a ministry leader. I think God has given me a gift for it.
- I have three friends I've been witnessing to, and our small group would be too big for them, so can we divide into two smaller groups, so they can come?

- Brian and Sue missed our group, so I called them to see if they're okay. Their kids are sick, so maybe our group can make meals for them. I'll start.
- Look at how many are at church today, it's awesome! The closest parking spot I could find was two blocks away! (Putman & Harrington, 2013, p. 67).

Helping a Spiritual Young Adult Move Forward:

- They need a place where they can learn how to serve. They need help to establish boundaries.
- They need a spiritual mentor to pray with, who will coach and debrief them on their ministry experiences.
- They need deep, ongoing relationships with people who offer encouragement and accountability.
- They need guidance in responding to the expectations of the people they serve.
- They need help identifying their gifts and developing their God given talents.
- When they get hurt, they need to process the pain, so they don't become disillusioned and cynical (Putman & Harrington, 2013, pp. 67-68).

Spiritual Parents Might Say:

- I wonder if God wants me to invest in Bill and help him mature in his faith.
- I want to help a person at work. They are asking me all sorts of questions about the world, God and what Jesus is-all-about. Pray for me as I show them my smart phone, *"3, 2, 1, You, the world and God"* (Unknown author, 2013).
- Peter and Sandy have been baptised today. When is the next *"GrowthWorks"* class? (North, 2010). Getting them into ministry, or into a small group is essential for their growth. Let's invite them to join our small group on Wednesday night.

- Our small group is going on a mission trip, down south in a few months.
- I want to be involved with the once-a-month Saturday night *"Storytelling Jesus' Story"* home group, as seen in Study 8 to 16. Later I would like to start up another once-a-month Saturday night home group.
- I want to be conscious of the influence my words and actions have when I go to the cinema with Brian and Sue. I get easily upset with movie plots. As new Christians, Brian and Sue are hungry for guidance, and I want to set an example for them.
- I have a spiritual young adult who is ready to be an apprentice leader in our group. It won't be long until we are ready to divide into two small groups.

Helping a Spiritual Parent Move Forward:

- They need to be mindful of the needs of the less mature disciples.
- They need to have close peer relationships with other spiritual parents (Putman & Harrington, 2013, pp. 70-71).
- They need a go-to-peer person to encourage them to hang in there.
- They need ongoing training to help sharpen their skills.
- They need to be trained in how to shrink and starve the Inner Critic with true word statements, as seen in the leaders' notes 12.
- They need to delegate responsibility to avoid burnout or worse deconstruct their faith and quit.
- They need to be encouraged and freed to make disciples in the church. They need the go-ahead to develop people to maturity.
- They need to be celebrated and honoured. When you celebrate spiritual parents, younger spiritual disciples will aspire to be like them (Putman & Harrington, 2013, pp. 70-71).

Reflection

(See Leaders' Notes 4a)

Spend 5 minutes as a group going over the previous few pages and answering the following questions.

Q: Do you recognise any of the key statements? Have you heard someone say them in the past?

____

____

____

Q: Have you ever said any of these key statements in the past? What spiritual stage is that?

____

____

____

Q: How could knowing this spiritual stage help you to develop and move forward?

____

____

____

A quick quiz

(See Leaders' Notes 5 for the answers).

What spiritual stage are these disciples at, and how can you help them move forward?

Q: Christians shouldn't listen to hip-hop or rock. That kind of music is just unchristian.

How are we going to help this person develop and move forward?

Q: I really want to go on a mission trip this summer. I know I'm ready for it. I know God has big plans for my life.

How are we going to help this person develop and move forward?

Q: I don't believe there is a God.

How are we going to help this person develop and move forward?

Q: Religion is a crutch for the weak

How are we going to help this person develop and move forward?

____

____

____

Q: I have a spiritual young adult who is ready to be an apprentice in our group; it won't be long until we are ready to branch off and multiply our small group.

How are we going to help this person develop and move forward?

____

____

____

Application – for Now and in the Future

Throughout the coming weeks, as you listen to people, identify the key statements that people say in each spiritual stage. Also, how will you help develop disciples and move people forward?

Prayer

Help us God to hear what spiritual stage people are at and to know what to say to help them to move forward. Give us the opportunity to share something we discovered with someone this week as a part of disciple making others to Christ.

Preparation for the Next Study

Go over several times, the lists of statements that people say in each stage of spiritual growth and how to help them move forward. And read Study 4.

MOVE FROM INFORMING TO PREPARING (PART 1)

A Quick Reminder

The disciple making path is influenced by *three* directional moves that must take place, if a church wants to become a disciple making community for Jesus.

1. Move from **disconnecting to connecting** (Mt 13:3–24).
      share to win, then connect

2. Move from **informing to preparing** (Mt 10; Lk 10; Eph 4:11–16).
      build to move

3. Move from **accumulating to sending** (Mk 6:7; Lk 10:1–3).
      train to send

Move From Disconnecting to Connecting

This direction helps us to move our thinking from being disconnected to people, to making disciples. To win spiritually dead people for Jesus, we should understand the Five Plus Five, the post-Christian society that we inhabit and that it's not all about evangelism.

Share to Win

As disciples of Christ, we should purposefully build relationships with non-Christians, people who are spiritually dead, as we once were (Eph 2:1–2), by being salt and light to the world (Mt 5:13–16), using a model that can be described as prayer, care and share. Remembering that Jesus is always with us (Mt 28:20), we share life together (1 Thess 2:8) through deeds and words, praying for people by name, caring for their heart-felt needs and doing acts of kindness (deeds) and by relating to them in conversation (words). This happens best in social environments, especially in environments that lead to sharing spiritual conversations with people who are open, and eventually sharing an invitation to hear the gospel message *"come and see"* (Jn 1:39), to check out the facts about who Jesus is. The main fact would be, Jesus is fully God and fully human, at the same time (Jn 1:1, 14, 41). A further fact would be, why are his teachings so inground into today's society? Jesus' teachings that are accepted into today's Western culture are, the equality of all people, care for the poor and marginalized, dignity of women and children, education and health care for everyone, forgiveness, democracy, being generous and being wise with money all have their beginnings in Jesus' teachings (Faase, 2016, p. 1). Then, an invitation to turn back to God and believe (Mt 4:17), and to follow Jesus (Jn 1:43) for a whole new fresh start in life (c.f. 2 Cor 3:16; 5:15).

Example 1. Topics of general and/or spiritual conversations could be on "the equality of all people, servant leadership, care for the poor and marginalized, the dignity of women and children, the importance of education and health care and the generosity of our wealth" (Faase, 2016, p. 1). These topics have their origin in Jesus' teaching, and they are an effective way to indirectly share about Jesus, as many Western ideologies stem from Jesus' teaching.

For example, you could show a person, who is open and willing, on your smart phone or tablet, a short YouTube video trailer from *Jesus the Game Changer* (Faase, 2016, June 29) or *Storytelling Jesus' Story – The Easter Story* (see Appendix 1). Then ask questions such as, What surprised you in the story? What would you say is the main idea in the story? If the story is true, how will you live differently?

Sure, most of these conversations with people may not go deep into theological realms, however it will be fulfilling a part of the Great Commission: "*...make disciples ... teaching them to obey everything I have commanded you.*" As you talk about the topics from *Jesus the Game Changer* or *Storytelling Jesus' Story* you are highlighting Jesus' teachings that are already a part of our culture. By doing this, you teach them about what God has already instructed and guide them to further knowledge and passion for Jesus.

The early apostles proclaimed the gospel and won disciples (Acts 14:21). As non-Christians respond and follow Jesus, through spiritual re-birth, they move from being spiritually dead, to becoming a spiritual infant (Heb 5:13). They are made alive in Christ (Col 2:13), being spiritually reborn – not by a physical birth but a birth that comes from God (Jn 1:13), who are *"born of God"* (1 Jn 3:9; 5:1), *"like newborn babies"* (1 Pt 2:2); someone who has put their trust in Jesus and become a disciple of Jesus, who move towards spiritual maturity (Col 1:28).

Then Connect

We help new disciples connect with other disciples (establishing ongoing relational connections), in relational environments. For example, having a coffee one-on-one or in a small group, or being involved in a church service or activity. These environments should concentrate on teaching people to obey the teaching of Jesus (Mt 28:20), by building disciple relationships like he did. It is important to connect them into a biblical, relational environment, for example Sunday church services for worship, and into small groups for fellowship (Acts 2:42–47).

John Finkelde (Blog, 2022) said a small group pastor in a megachurch told him that 93 percent of new people in their church left within 12 months if they did not begin serving or join a small group. Obviously, the percentage is lower in smaller churches. This disciple making material could be taught in another small group of new disciples or one-on-one with someone.

This Study's Focus. 2:
Move from Informing to Preparing

The next move that churches need to make is to prepare people for works of service (Titus 3:14) and not just informing people about how to be Christians. It starts with a pastor or a small group leader living his or her life as a disciple maker for Jesus Christ. Jesus interacted at different levels with different people groups, making disciples in four different disciple making relational environments.

The Inner Circle Relationships

Jesus had close disciple making relationships (one leader personally interacting with two or three people). Jesus was much closer to Peter, James and John (who became his *inner circle*), and he invested quality time in them. He shared with these three men, and modelled the deepest level of intentional, relational disciple making. His insight, wisdom and approach had an enormous impact on them, and they became the first leaders of the early church (Putman & Harrington, 2013, p. 107).

Personal Relationships

Jesus also had personal disciple making relationships (one leader interacting with up to 16 people). Jesus led a larger group of 12 to 16 people (Lk 8:1–3), whom he personally discipled in relational environments. Not all of them were intimately close to him, but they still had a quality relationship, and spent regular time together. Working with the twelve disciples was the focus of much of his ministry and discipleship. He poured into their lives, and they learnt how to minister with him to others.

Ten to twelve people is a sizeable number for a church, mid-week small group. The group leader knows the group and their personal lives and struggles and helps them to follow Jesus in today's context. The group knows the leader's life and struggles too, as they do life together (Putman & Harrington, 2013, pp. 107-108). The small group leader may have a possible future leader, or a second-in-charge, a peer spiritual parent in the group as well a go-to-person as the leader's inner circle. Together the small group leader and the inner circle care for the rest of the group.

Larger groups (20 to 30 people) for example, youth, men's, ladies, or senior groups. The main leader, the second-in-charge, and the two or three inner circle leaders, lead smaller groups (five to seven people), at the study discussion time. Smaller groups provide a better "peer-to-peer discussion" while "removing any perceived teacher–student hierarchy" (Chan, 2018, p. 181). It also gives the group the confidence to speak up and participate. The leaders of these smaller groups get to know the group better, can help them in their personal lives and help them to follow Jesus toward spiritual maturity. The smaller group gets to know the leader's life and struggles too, as they all follow Jesus together.

We will look at the other two different disciple making relational environment in the next study.

Bible Reading

Read Matthew 10:5–23. Pray that God will speak to you through his Word. Spend ten minutes going over the passage and answer the following questions.

(See Leaders' Notes 6)

Q: What do you notice for the first time? What stood out to you?

____

____

Q: As you think about this Bible passage what do you wonder about? What questions does it raise?

____

____

Q: What might this passage reveal to us about God or Jesus and his work, or plans?

____

____

Application – For Now and in the Future

Q: If this passage is true, how will it change or move your thinking?

____

____

In Preparation for Studies 8 to 16

This study material will go through 9 studies of storytelling Jesus' story, (See Leaders' Notes 7). Missionaries all over the world successfully use storytelling the gospel message to connect with the people they work with. Missionaries who work in universities understand most international students prefer learning from stories. Think about it: stories make up the biggest portion of the Bible with 40 percent of the Old Testament and 60 percent of the New Testament (Lawrence, 2010, p. 45). And Jesus told stories and parables too. Today, storytelling really works as a disciple making tool.

Rick Sessoms (2012, April 12) states, "70% of all the people in the world today", which is about two out of three are "oral learners". Oral learners prefer learning from stories. They like to observe, hear and learn how ideas and issues work through stories.

Therefore, if we want to reach people for Jesus, we should story tell Jesus' stories.

Stories connect complex thoughts by breaking them down into easier forms. Complex thoughts, ideas and beliefs are broken down without using the words for these thoughts, ideas and beliefs (e.g., the complex idea of brokenness and sin), which can be broken down to its central element. By using God's resources of life (relationships, food, money, the environment), but living at a distance from God. We may not live 'wildly' but we do live 'separately' from the Father (Lk 15:11–32). When my wife told a person about this definition of "sin," they got it straight away.

Stories get the listener to see through the worldview of the story (Chan, 2020, p. 97). Even though sin is living separately from God, according to the story of the lost son in Luke 15:11–32, when we turn back to God, He is a searching, running, embracing, pardoning, lavishing, forgiving parent.

Stories invite the listener to postpone disbelief suitable to the genre of the story. In the same way, when storytelling the gospel or a passage from the Bible, the listener is asked to postpone their disbelief regarding Jesus' miracles and rising from the dead, because of the genre of the gospel story (Chan, 2018, p. 177).

We believe that the one and only primary pursuit in disciple making is speaking God's Word. Re-telling (or speaking), a small part of God's Word through one of Jesus' stories is a terrific way to share the gospel message. Remember, this is all about linking their story line into Jesus' story line, so they can have a better ending to their life story, forever.

How to Story Tell Jesus' Stories

Each person in your small group is going to retell one of the Bible stories through studies 8 to 16. This is an opportunity to start preparing and memorizing their particular story from the Bible. On that night, the group will not read the Bible passage. The designated person will retell the passage in their own words. This is not about memorizing the story, word-for-word from the Bible. It is about remembering the scenes from the Bible story and then retelling those scenes. It is important to use language that the listener and you would be comfortably using in an ordinary conversation (Chan, 2018, p. 179). The purpose is to retell Jesus' story using the **SCR** abbreviation, **Simple, Correct and Remarkable.**

Simple

Simple means presenting your story that is easily understood, by keeping the language simple and clearly understandable. Avoid church language or jargon and use easily understood words, as suggested here, for example.

Use these words	Instead of these words
Place of worship or religious places	Synagogue or temple
Religious leader	Pharisee
Brokenness or falling short	Sin
Being made right with God	Righteous
Turning back to God	Repentance
The good news story	The Gospel
The inner critic	The devil
Telling or teaching	Preaching
This is my teaching	Jesus' commands
Live in me or make your home in me	Abide in me

Correct

Simplify the story by leaving out some details, (e.g., town or city names, people's names, location details) but do not attach other details to enhance the story. You do not want to change the content and the meaning of the passage.

Remarkable

Restate the drama of the story in a memorable manner using facial expressions, body language and hand gestures. You can also use makeshift costumes, backdrops with pictures and printed titles, or green screens with projected images.

Think Like a Translator

Our aim is to put the story in a new form, to speak the language of the hearer. We want to communicate Jesus' stories in a more understandable form although retain the original concepts, as a translator would do from one language to another. We are taking the story that was meant for a Greco-Roman, first century Palestine audience to the present-day audience. Our desire is to speak a fresh and clear word to the modern context, without seriously changing the content of the story (Erickson, 1985, p. 113).

Writing the Script

Search your particular passage on the internet, using the Message (MSG) or The Living Bible (TLB). Cut and paste the Bible passage into a document, change some of the difficult language to easily understood ones. Tweak particular sentences to the way you would normally say them. Add an introduction such as: "Now, this is how the birth of Jesus came about," for the Christmas story, or for the Easter story you could say, "With trumped up charges they arrested Jesus, the perfect man, beat him and led him away to be crucified." The conclusion could include a summary such as: "This is the real Christmas story of Jesus' birth to his early childhood", or for the Easter story, "John wrote this down so that you may believe that Jesus is the Messiah, the Son of God, and by believing in Jesus you can have eternal life in heaven". For further examples see the YouTube videos, "Phillip Matthews' Storytelling Jesus' Story" as seen in Appendix 1.

Video Your Story

As an outreach, take a video of all the stories and, with comments and questions, post them on your Facebook page or other social media that you use. Interact with comments that people post in response. See it as an outreach opportunity. Place these videos onto your phone ready to show someone who is asking questions.

Schedule for Group Members to Story Tell Jesus' Story

Study 8 – The Christmas Story: God has Moved into the Neighborhood.

Chronologically through the following passages: Luke 1:26–38; Matthew 1:18-25; Luke 2:1–32; Matthew 2:1–21 and Luke 2:39–52.

Small Group person No. 1: The leader_______________________.

Date:____

Study 9 – Jesus' First Followers: Come, See and Follow Jesus.

Chronologically through the following passages: John 1:35–46; Luke 5:1–11; Matthew 9:9–13; Luke 6:12–16.

Small Group person No. 2: _______________________.

Date:____

Study 10 – The Lost Animal, Lost Money and the Lost Son - Search and Rescue.

Luke 15:1–31.

Small Group person No. 3: _______________________________.

Date:____

Study 11 – Jesus, the Blind Man and Zacchaeus: Heals and Restores.

Luke 18:35-19:10. Parallel passages: Matthew 20:29–34; Mark 10:46–52.

Small Group person No. 4: _______________________________.

Date:____

Study 12 – Jesus Heals the Paralytic: Forgiveness.

Matthew 4:23–25 and Mark 2:1–12. Parallel passages: Matthew 9:1–8; Luke 5:17–26.

Small Group person No. 5: _______________________________.

Date:____

Study 13 – Jesus Calms a Storm and Heals the Demoniac: Heals and Restores.

Luke 8:22–39. Parallel passages: Matthew 8:18, 23–27; Mark 4:35–41.

Small Group person No. 6:_______________________________.

Date:____

Study 14 – Jesus Heals the Woman Hemorrhaging for 12 years.

Your faith has made you well. Mark 5:21 and 24–34. Parallel passages: Matthew 9:20–22 and Luke 8:42b–48.

Small Group person No. 7: ________________________________.

Date:____

Study 15 – Jesus is the Way, the Truth and the Life. The Only Trustworthy Path to Heaven.

John 14:1–15.

Small Group person No. 8:____________________________.

Date:____

Study 16 – The Easter Story

Jesus' crucifixion, death, burial, and resurrection. Chronologically through the following passages: Matthew 27:33–66 and John 20:1–29; 1 Cor 15:6; John 20:30–31.

Small Group person No. 9: The Leader ___________________.

Date:____

For more information for studies 8 to 16, see Leaders' Notes 7.

Prayer

Heavenly Father, will you give us an opportunity to share with someone this week, as a part of disciple making others to Christ and to prepare for storytelling Jesus' story and to be ready to retell it on the date that has been allocated to you.

Preparation for the Next Study

Review the notes on how to story tell Jesus' story and prepare your story. Have a look at Leaders' Notes 7. Preview Study 5.

MOVE FROM INFORMING TO PREPARING (PART 2)

JESUS INTERACTED AT DIFFERENT DISCIPLE MAKING levels with diverse people groups. Jesus discipled people in four different disciple making relational environments. In the last study we looked at *the inner circle relationships* and the *personal relationships.*

The Inner Circle Relationships

Close disciple making relationships (one leader personally interacting with two or three people). Jesus was much closer to Peter, James and John (who became his *inner circle*), and he invested quality time in them. He shared with these three men, and modelled the deepest level of intentional, relational disciple making. His insight, wisdom and approach had an enormous impact on them, and they became the first leaders of the early church (Putman & Harrington, 2013, p. 107).

Personal Relationships

Jesus also had personal disciple making relationships (one leader interacting with up to 16 people). Jesus led a larger group of 12 to 16 people (Lk 8:1–3), whom he personally discipled in relational environments. Not all of them were intimately close to him, but they still had a quality relationship, and spent regular time together. Working with the twelve disciples was the focus of much of his ministry and discipleship. He poured into their lives, and they learnt how to minister with him to others.

Ten to twelve people is a sizeable number for a church, mid-week small group. The group leader knows the group and their personal lives and struggles and helps them to follow Jesus in today's context. The group knows the leader's life and struggles too, as they do life together (Putman & Harrington, 2013, pp. 107-108). The small group leader may have a possible future leader, or a second-in-charge, a peer spiritual parent in the group as well a go-to-person as the leader's inner circle. Together the small group leader and the inner circle care for the rest of the group.

Larger groups (20 to 30 people), youth for example. The main leader, the second-in-charge, and the two or three inner circle leaders, lead smaller groups (five to seven people), at the study discussion time. Smaller groups provide a better "peer-to-peer discussion" while "removing any perceived teacher–student hierarchy" (Chan, 2018, p. 181). It also gives the group the confidence to speak up and participate. The leaders of these smaller groups get to know the group better, can help them in their personal lives and help them to follow Jesus toward spiritual maturity. The smaller group gets to know the leader's life and struggles too, as they all follow Jesus together.

This Studies Focus: Social and Public Relationships

Jesus related at different disciple making levels, with diverse people groups, in varied relational environments. In this study we will look at disciple making in *social relationships* and *public relationships*.

Social Relationships

Social disciple making relationships (one leader interacting with up to 120 people). Jesus had significant social relationships with Mary, Martha, Lazarus, Bartimaeus, Zacchaeus, Matthew, Peter's mother-in-law, just to name a few. He also had relationships with a group called the seventy-two (Lk 10:17). Jesus invested time in these men before he sent them out to make disciples in his name. Seventy-two grew to one hundred and twenty, who later met in the upper room when God's Spirit was poured out, on the day of Pentecost (Acts 1:15). At this level people know each other by name, and they may know a few personal details about one another.

Throughout history, most churches have been around this size, and it should be no surprise to learn that 120 is an ideal size for a group of people who want to work together for Jesus along his disciple making path. Keep in mind that within a group this big, the small group leader, gifted teacher, or pastor, will also be disciple making with smaller groups of (5 to 7 people) and larger groups of (10 to 16 people), as well as closer disciple making relationships between groups of (3 people), the leader's inner circle (Putman & Harrington, 2013, p. 108). The small group leader or pastor will be on the lookout for possible future leaders, or they may be training a possible future leader, or groups of future leaders for **ministry.**

Public Relationships

Public disciple making relationships (one leader interacting with larger crowds of people). In large public gatherings of people, Jesus discipled people publicly, speaking to assorted sizes of crowds. At this level, Jesus would teach God's Word, God's love, explain the realities of turning back to God, finding forgiveness, the close personal relationship as God's children and eternal life in heaven. At this level of relational disciple making, church leaders interact with a large crowd of people. They set the vision, imparting the basic DNA of what it means to follow Jesus. This is also where leaders and gifted teachers will speak about the realities of love, kindness, being genuine and transparent and, most importantly, a commitment to Jesus, the cross and disciple making.

Today, public gatherings could be one leader interacting with larger number of people on the internet. Interacting with people on the internet is an important component of Jesus' disciple making path to the corporate relationships if they are authentic and Christ-centred. At this level, pastors, gifted teachers, and small group leaders, can model in their teaching and personal stories what it means to be a follower of Christ. There is good research to show that this is the level at which many lost people first learn what it means to be a disciple of Jesus (Benson, *Discipleship in a Digital Age*). Later, move towards spiritual maturity, as they walk through the *three main directives* and the *increasing* features of Jesus' disciple making path.

Bible Reading

(See Leaders' Notes 8)

Read Luke 10. Pray that God will speak to you through his Word. Spend 10 minutes going over the passage and answer the following questions.

Q: What do you notice for the first time? What stood out to you?

Q: As you think about this passage, what do you wonder about? What questions does this passage raise?

Q: What might this passage reveal to us about God/Jesus, his work, his plan?

Application – For Now and in the Future

Spend 5 minutes in preparation for the application for this passage. In one sentence, write down one aspect of what you learnt from this passage. After share with the group:

Prayer

Pray that God will give you an opportunity to share your discovery with someone this week as a part of disciple making others to Christ. And please help us to prepare and memorize the Bible passage and be ready to retell it on the date that has been allocated to us from study 8 to study 16.

Preparation for the Next Study

Work through the recap for Study 6. Prepare, memorize and rehearse your story ready for Study 8 to Study 16.

MOVE FROM INFORMING TO PREPARING (PART 3)

A Quick Recap:

Move from **disconnecting** to **connecting** is a move in our thinking from being disconnected to people, to reaching out to people, to make disciples. To win spiritually dead people for Jesus, then help new disciples connect with other disciples. This changes our character as a growing follower of Jesus.

Share to Win

All disciples of Christ should purposefully build relationships with non-Christians, people who are spiritually dead (Eph 2:1–2), by being *salt* and *light* (Mt 5:13–16). Remembering that Jesus is always with us (Mt 28:20), we do this by sharing life together (1 Thess 2:8), through *deeds* and *words*. Jesus' example to us was, he went teaching the good news of God's family, through (*words*) and doing acts of kindness (*deeds*) (Mt 9:35).

Praying for them by name, looking for opportunities to care for them. People share what is important to them by having general conversations. This happens best in social relational environments or social networks or social groups in society, such as neighbours, in workplaces, sport clubs, community groups, friends and family. These groups are a unique circle of influence, a place where you are an insider who is readily accepted within the group (Putman & Harrington, 2013, p. 93). Relational environments could also be you and another Christian friend taking someone to the beach or a café for an hour every second week.

These environments hopefully lead to spiritual conversations, which could be on topics from the video, *Jesus the Game Changer*, looking at Jesus' teaching that have deeply influenced Western society. For example, the equality of all, servant leadership, care for the poor and marginalised, dignity of women and children, education, forgiveness, to name just a few (Faase, 2016, p. 1). In the beginning of the conversation, they probably will have no idea you are sharing about Jesus.

Eventually provide an invitation to hear the gospel message, *"come and see"* (Jn 1:39), then *"repent and believe"* (Mt 4:17; Jn 3:36) and *"come follow"* Jesus (Jn 1:43). For example, you could show a person who is open and willing a short YouTube video such as, *Storytelling Jesus' Story – The Easter Story* on your smart phone or tablet (see Appendix 1). Then ask questions like, What surprised you in the story? What would you say is the main idea in the story? If the story is true, how will you live differently? Alternatively, a Christian friend and you could use the DVDs *Jesus the Game Changer* (Faase, 2016) or *LifeWorks* (North, 2015) or *Christianity Explained* (Bennett, 2004), one-on-one, or in a group of four (two Christians and two unbelievers).

The early apostles proclaimed the gospel and won disciples (Acts 14:21). As people respond and follow Jesus, the non-Christian moves from being spiritually dead to becoming a spiritual infant (Heb 5:13). They are made alive in Christ (Col 2:13), being spiritually reborn *of God* (1 Jn 3:9; 5:1), *"like newborn babies"* (1 Pt 2:2).

A new believer can be described as a spiritual infant, someone who has put their trust in Jesus and become a disciple of Jesus. As Matthew 4:19 shows, they follow Jesus and are changed by Jesus. They are then committed to the mission of Jesus by reaching out into the community, making disciples who make other disciples, simultaneously moving towards spiritual maturity (Mt 28:19–20).

Then Connect

We help new disciples connect with other disciples (establishing ongoing relational connections) in relational environments (Acts 2:42–47). For example, having a coffee one-on-one or in a small group, or being involved in a church service or activity. These environments should concentrate on teaching people to obey Jesus' teachings (Mt 28:20), by building disciple relationships like he did. It is important to connect them into a biblical relational environment, for example a church service for worship, and small groups for fellowship. Remember that earlier example from a megachurch: if new people were not connected into small groups or involved in service, up to 93 percent of them could leave the church within 12 months. Thus, it is important to teach people to move towards spiritual maturity and disciple making. This disciple making material is also most effective in a small group of new disciples.

Church as a Team

We need churches that have small groups. Jesus discipled in small groups. Small groups provide an effective platform to teach people, for them to ask questions, to check for understanding, and to view the leader's teaching style. We do not want to lecture people, because only 20 percent of people have an auditory learning style, and we do not want fake classroom learning styles.

Jesus discipled in small groups, and he did that for a purpose. Small groups provide accountability because they are relational by nature. The ability to look into someone's eyes and know that they understand is a unique aspect of a small group setting. There are also opportunities for a person to develop in a small group, or to learn how to lead. We also learn how to pastor people, by doing so in a small group. You cannot get good at something, unless you give it a go. Small groups are where people are led, taught, made accountable in relationships, and can develop as active Christians. You cannot develop properly by sitting on the bench, watching someone else live an active Christian life. You yourself have to take action.

The Bible states in Ephesians 4:11–16, God gives the church gifted leaders, pastor's teachers, apostles, prophets, and evangelists, to prepare God's people for works of service, to build up the community of believers, until we all reach maturity. God has called all of us to ministry, which are *works of service* (Eph 4:12). It is about leaders training up people for ministry, then releasing them as an army into the community, who live for Christ and make disciples. When God's people are released to play, everyone on the team plays, and everyone understands their job. This fulfills the Great Commission, to go into the world and make disciples. Our job is to get the team to play, and when they do so, we win. If we go back to the way the early church operated, we will have the impact that they did.

Bible Reading

(See Leaders' Notes 9)

Read Ephesians 4:11-16. Pray that God will speak to you through his Word. Spend five minutes going over the passage and answer the following questions.

Q: What do you notice for the first time? What stood out to you?

Q: As you think about this passage, what do you wonder about? What questions does it raise?

Q: What might this passage reveal to us about God/Jesus, his work, his plan?

This Study's Focus. 2:
Move From Informing to Preparing

Leaders and mature spiritual parents, mentor or coaches need to make a move from giving people more information to preparing and equipping them for transformation. We want to raise up people for works of service so that the community of Christ may be built up (Eph 4:12).

Build

Building committed disciples who grow towards maturity. Initially, they grow from spiritual infants to spiritual children or *"little children"* (1 Jn 2:12). A spiritual child has a sense of belonging and community, they want to exalt Christ (in worship), deepening their relationship with him through regular devotions, prayer, Bible reading and study. They deepen their relationships within the Church community (fellowship), as they purposefully build relationships with non-Christians, and other believers, at all levels of spiritual maturity. This occurs in both social and biblical environments. They expect spiritually mature believers to help them discover their spiritual gifts, and usually accept being involved in the church service, ministries, or other church activities. They also understand that by reaching out to unbelievers and serving (using their gifts, talents, and money), they too are moving towards maturity.

To Move

Disciples should always be moving forward, and never backwards. The next move is from being a spiritual child, to becoming a spiritual young adult, both male and female (1 Jn 2:13b, 14c). This is a part of building and equipping people to become mature believers, eventually making disciples, in biblical, relational environments. A spiritual young adult maintains a greater sense of community (fellowship) and exalting Christ (worship), digging deeper into their relationship with Christ (regular and longer devotions, prayers, Bible studies and reading Christian literature). They deepen their relationships within the Church community (fellowship), in both small groups and the Sunday service. They purposefully build relationships with other believers, at all levels of spiritual maturity. They expect spiritually mature believers to help them discover their spiritual gifts, to be involved in service, e.g., ministry, outreach, and other church community activities.

Spiritual young adults also purposefully build relationships with non-Christians to win spiritually dead people for Jesus. This occurs in both social and biblical environments. They purposefully build relationships with infant believers and help care for them. They are heading towards maturity. They understand and accept that reaching out to unbelievers (spiritually dead people) and caring for spiritual infants helps move them towards maturity.

Reflection

In groups of two or three, go over a few "Recognizing key phrases that people say in each stage," and "Helping the person develop and move forward," from Study 3.

**Q: Have you heard yourself in any of these phrases? What spiritual
level is that?**

**Q: Are you at the same spiritual level that you thought you were in
study one? If not, how are you going to get to the next spiritual
stage towards maturity?**

Note: When a spiritual child starts to make disciples, who make disciples, they
start to move into being a spiritual young adult very quickly. This is evident in
Ephesians 4:14-16 and 1 John 2:12-13. Being not mentally *"lazy"* or *"slow to
learn"* is the key (Heb 5:11, 6:12).

Q: Have you heard any of these phrases over the past few weeks?

**Q: Is it getting easier to recognise key phrases that people say in
each stage, and to help the person develop and move forward?**

Application – For Now and in the Future

Spend 5 mins in preparation for the application and after share with the group.

Q: How are you going to move from disconnecting to connecting?

\
\
\

Q: How are you going to move from informing to preparing?

\
\
\

Q: Are you committed to growing towards spiritually maturity?

\
\
\

See also 1 Cor 13:11; 14:20; Col 4:12; Phil 3:15; Jms 1:4.

Q: Are you committed to helping spiritual children move to spiritual young adults?

Yes / No

Helping spiritual children to move from being self-centered, to being God-centered by reorienting their lives around God's Word, his people and Jesus' mission of making disciples, helps them move along the maturity path towards becoming a spiritual young adult.

Prayer

We pray to build committed disciples who grow towards maturity who help spiritual children move to spiritual young adults and then onto spiritual parents. Pray that God will give you an opportunity to share your discovery with someone this week as a part of attracting others to Christ. And please help us to prepare and memorize the Bible passage and be ready to retell it on the date that has been allocated to us from study 8 to study 16.

Preparation for Next Study

Work through the recap for Study 7. Prepare, memorize and rehearse your story ready for Study 8 to Study 16.

MOVE FROM ACCUMULATING TO SENDING

Recap with Some Added Examples:

Move from **disconnecting** to **connecting** is a move in our thinking from being disconnected to people, to reaching out to people, to make disciples. To win spiritually dead people for Jesus, then help new disciples connect with other disciples. This changes our character as a growing follower of Jesus.

Share to Win

All followers of Christ should purposefully build relationships with non-Christians, people who are *"spiritually dead"* (Eph 2:1), by being salt and light. We do this by sharing life together (1 Thes 2:8), through *deeds* and *words*. People today want action and deeds more than just words. However, we need to use words, actions and deeds. It is the example Jesus gave us: he went preaching the good news of the kingdom (*words*) and doing acts of kindness (*actions and deeds*) (Mt 9:35). Remember that Jesus is always with us (Mt 28:20), and use Jesus' model of prayer, care and share. Pray for people by name, looking for opportunities to care for them and sharing life with them by having general conversations. This happens best in social environments, especially in environments that lead to spiritual conversations and eventually an invitation to hear the gospel message *come and see* (Jn 1:39) or check out the facts about who Jesus is. Jesus' message is *repent and believe* (Mt 4:17; Jn 3:36) and *come follow* Jesus (Jn 1:43).

Author's personal examples: On the last day of my 4-week stint as a casual mowing temp, in the parks and gardens of a local council, I was reflecting on the fact that I had not done much disciple making during that time. I was thinking about useful ways of disciple making, that do not involve preaching to others. For example, I would not want to just listen to a Christian pod cast on the way to work and talk to my coworkers about it afterwards. It would not work.

After reflecting for a while, I realized I had a couple of conversations over the past 4 weeks, with my co-workers. I talked about caring for others, equality of all people, all people have value and servant leadership. They probably had no idea I was sharing indirectly about Jesus. Sure, most of these conversations with my co-workers did not go very deep. However, when they asked me, I said, "Yes, I have faith in Jesus." In doing this, I understood I was fulfilling a part of the Great Commission. *"Therefore, go and make disciples ... and teaching them to obey everything I have commanded you."* You see, the verb, "go," has the meaning of "as you go." What Jesus is saying is make disciples as you go through life. When you are at work, you should make disciples. By talking about topics related to teachings that Jesus left us, others can agree with the values spoken about and come to a knowledge of Jesus Christ, because these values are a part of our culture (see examples from the video, *Jesus the Game Changer*). To me, this looks very much like *"teaching them to obey everything I have commanded you."*

I hear you ask how does this work. Here are two conversations with Clive and Stan. Clive commented that you can have bad experiences with Christians, and good ones. He acknowledged a well-known local charity and the leader of that charity as a good bloke. Clive then said, "But the others are all born again nut jobs." As he looked straight at me, remembering I am a follower of Christ, he said, "Well not all of them." I thought to myself that he meant I am not a born again nut job. That has got to be a good thing, I suppose. If we can give non-believers a positive experience with Christians, it can lead them to an interest in Christ, and eventually redemption.

The other conversation with Stan was somewhat hilarious. He was wearing a backpack with weed poison and said to me, "I'm going to pray." Well, that is what I thought he said. Realizing my mistake, I started to sing M.C. Hammer's song, "We got to pray just to make it through the day." Well, I hope that did not spoil my reputation as someone who's not a "born again nut job."

Yet, my prayer is that when Stan next picks up a spray pack to spray some weeds, that the song, "we got to pray just to make it through the day," would remind him about prayer, and to whom the prayer appeals. Hopefully, one day, this leads to faith in Jesus. For Clive, I pray that he will have more positive Christian experiences and find Christ in the future. Both of these examples illustrate how general conversations and building relationships are a valid strategy to win others to Christ.

The early apostles proclaimed the gospel and won disciples (Acts 14:21). Win means, introduce them to Jesus, by persuading them about God's love for them, to return back to God for a whole new fresh start in life. Here a non-Christian respond and follows Jesus who moves from being spiritually dead to becoming a spiritual infant (Heb 5:13), who is *"born of God"* (1 Jn 3:9; 5:1), a newborn baby (1 Pt 2:2), and alive in Christ (Col 2:13).

A new believer can be described as a person who has a new life (Rom 6:4), who is a spiritual infant; someone who has put their trust in Jesus and become a disciple of Jesus. As we find in Matthew 4:19, they follow Jesus (head level) and are changed by Jesus (heart level). They are then committed to the mission of Jesus (hands on level) by reaching out into the community, making disciples who make other disciples, simultaneously moving towards spiritual maturity (Mt 28:19–20).

Then Connect

We help new disciples connect with other disciples by establishing ongoing relational connections Acts 2:42–47). For example, having a coffee one-on-one or in a small group, or being involved in a church service or activity. These environments should concentrate on teaching people to obey the teaching of Jesus (Mt 28:20), by building disciple relationships like he did. It is important to connect them into a biblical, relational environment, for example a church service for worship, and into small groups for fellowship. Remember an earlier example from a megachurch: if new people were not connected into small groups or involved in service, up to 93 percent of them could leave the church within 12 months. Thus, it is important to teach people to move towards spiritual maturity and discipleship making.

Move from **informing** to **preparing** is the next move that leaders and mature spiritual parents, mentor or coaches need to make is a move from giving people more information to preparing and equipping them for transformation. We want to raise up people for works of service so that the community of Christ may be built up (Eph 4:12).

Build

Committed disciples grow towards maturity. Initially, they grow from spiritual infants to spiritual children (1 Jn 2:12, 14, 18, 28). A spiritual child has a sense of belonging and community, they want to exalt Christ (worship him), and deepen their relationship with him through regular devotions, prayer and Bible readings. They deepen their relationships within the Church through fellowship, as they purposefully build relationships with non-Christians, and other believers, at all levels of spiritual maturity. This occurs in both social and biblical environments. They expect spiritually mature believers to help them discover their spiritual gifts, and usually accept being involved in the church service, ministries or other church activities. They also understand that by reaching out to unbelievers and serving (using their gifts, talents and money), they too are moving towards maturity. Note that in the beginning, spiritual parents allow spiritual infants and spiritual children to depend on them, but as they grow, spiritual parents teach them to place their dependence onto God.

To Move

Disciples should always be moving forward, never backwards. The next move is from being a spiritual child, to becoming a spiritual young adult (1 Jn 2:13b, 14c). This is a part of building and equipping people to become mature believers, eventually making disciples in biblical, relational environments. A spiritual young adult maintains a greater sense of community through fellowship and by exalting Christ in worship and digging deeper into their relationship with Christ through regular and longer devotions, prayers, Bible studies and reading Christian literature. They deepen their relationships within the church through fellowship, in both small groups and church services. They purposefully build relationships with other believers at all levels of spiritual maturity. They expect spiritually mature believers to help them discover their spiritual gifts and to be involved in service in ministry, outreach and other church activities.

Spiritual young adults also purposefully build relationships with non-Christians to win spiritually dead people for Jesus. This occurs in both social and biblical environments. They purposefully build relationships with infant believers and help care for them. They are heading towards maturity. They understand and accept that reaching out to unbelievers (spiritually dead people) and caring for spiritual infants helps move them towards maturity.

This Study's Focus. 3: Move from Accumulating to Sending

The third and last area that church communities need to make, is a move in their purpose. A move from accumulating large numbers of people and keeping them, to sending people out into the wider community doing what Jesus did. *"As you sent me into the world, I have sent them into the world"* (John 17:18). *Jesus said, "Peace be with you! As the Father has sent me, I am sending you"* (John 20:21).

"Whoever believes in me will do the works I have been doing, and they will do even greater things than these, because I am going to the Father" (Jn 14:12).

Train to Send Out

Disciples that make disciples are moving from being spiritual young adults to being younger spiritual parents (1 Jn 2:13, 14b). Younger parent believers are like older siblings who help other mature parents care for spiritual infants and children, in their walk with Christ. The spiritual infant or child follows the example of the spiritual parent as they follow the example of Jesus (1 Cor 11:1; Eph 5:1). Young spiritual parents expect that spiritually mature leaders might invite them to be trained as disciple workers – increasing workers for the harvest (Lk 10:2; Mt 9:38), ultimately serving the needs of the church family and the wider community as harvest workers. A wonderful way to serve the wider community as harvest workers would be using the *Storytelling the Disciple Making Path* material in another small group of new disciples, giving them a great start in their walk with Christ, moving them towards spiritual maturity.

These people are leaders who make other leaders as exemplified by Paul and Timothy. This is the fourth spiritual stage, where disciples transition from being young spiritual parents, to spiritually mature parents (Eph 4:13–15). A spiritually mature parent is like a foster parent who seeks out infant and child believers, sharing, feeding, caring for them, and coaching them towards maturity. Spiritually mature leaders train potential leaders as apprentices, towards future ministry service as a small group leader or some other ministry leader. They can also lead them to a role where they mentor (coach) spiritual infant and child believers to move towards maturity. They could also become a small group leader's peer-support person, someone that the leader can go to and bounce ideas off. Ultimately, this serves the needs of the church family, and the wider community. Each ministry leader then multiplies themselves and their ministry when they use the apprentice and coach model.

Mature spiritual parents (mentor or coaches) increase disciples to form other small groups, and other ministries, ultimately serving the needs of the church family community and the wider community. This might occur both in your home country or overseas. At home, for example, when a small group grows from 10 to 12 people, the group could branch into two. Both groups could meet in the same house, but in two different rooms if needed.

These people are leaders who make other leaders who also increase their ministry, like John with the seven churches in the first three chapters in Revelations. It is the same with us today: as God the Father has sent Jesus into the world, Jesus has sent us into the world to make disciples (Jn 17:18). But today, what would this potentially look like?

Small Group Members

Pray at 10.02 a.m. or at 9.38 p.m. for the harvest, the harvest workers and to be involved in the harvest (as a reflection on Luke 10:2 and Matthew 9:38 passages). Do that for 12 months or more and see what happens. Be encouraged to go and make disciples, starting where people are at. God's calling to the churches is to make disciples (to trust and follow Jesus). This is where you, a devoted disciple, attracts people from outside the church, because of the change others see in your Christ-like life. The disciple making path empowers Christians to be more like Christ, as you intentionally develop relationships with non-believers in your social networks. You are also encouraged to go through this material *Storytelling the Disciple Making Path* with a spiritual infant or spiritual child, one-on-one, moving them towards spiritual maturity.

Pastors, Ministry Leaders and Small Group Leaders

As the pastor or small group leader, be on the lookout for an apprentice (a future small group leader) to train to step up into leadership when your small group grows larger. As you branch into two small groups, one group could have five to six people stay with the original leader, and the second group could have three to four people who are sent out with the new leader to form another group. These two groups could stay under the same roof as each other, coming together at the beginning of the night and for supper at the end of the night. The overflow group may study the same biblical material, as the original leader, as he or she coaches the younger leader, but eventually both leaders could study different biblical material, as led by the Lord.

However, the second group may encounter a situation where a family would like to host a small group. This means that they can move location, adding another two people to the group (the hosts). Both leaders are increasing their ministry in the future, as they invite and train potential future leaders (apprentices) and form small-group leaders and peer support networks (such as a go-to-person, or coach).

As well as sending out believers to multiply disciples, leaders should purposefully build relationships with non-Christians. This occurs by sharing life, to win spiritually dead people for Jesus and to connect spiritual infants and children to long-lasting relationships in biblical environments. These environments concentrate on teaching obedience to the teachings of Jesus (Mt 28:20), thus building disciple making relationships as Jesus did. The first phase of spiritual maturity is when a committed disciple transitions from spiritual infants to children. The second phase is the transition from being spiritual children to spiritual young adults. In this phase, the believer is trained to be a disciple who makes disciples. The third phase is to move from spiritual young adult to spiritual young parent by following the apprentice and coach model, sending out disciples to make disciples.

Why Do We Do This?

We do this to produce a disciple making movement. We want to create a movement of mature disciple makers, (increasing spiritual mature disciples for Christ). A disciple of Jesus is someone who follows Jesus at the head level, is being changed by Jesus at the heart level and is committed to the mission of Jesus at the practical level (increasing oneself) as they accept the call to action. They live out a lifestyle of "sentness". The word, "sentness" was the name Jesus gave to his disciples, as he renamed them "apostles" (Mk 3:14). The word, "apostle" means, someone sent out with authority on behalf of the Sender (Jesus) who is accountable to him (Harrison, p. 71). Therefore, some of these disciples became leaders who made other leaders (*increasing leaders and one's ministry*). By doing this, some of the disciples became coaches, mentors and others became peer supporters, to help care for spiritual infants and children, moving them towards spiritual maturity. This process follows a complex, linear progression from being spiritually dead, to becoming spiritual infants, then spiritual children, spiritual young adults, next and finally, spiritual mature parents. This is a vital process, as too many Christians stay in the spiritual infant or child stage for years, never spiritually maturing (Heb 5:12–6:1a), because they have become mentally "*lazy*" and "*slow to learn*" (Heb 5:11, 6:12).

Bible Reading

(See Leaders' Notes 10)

Read Hebrews 5:11–6:12. Pray that God will speak to you through his word. Spend 5 to 6 minutes going over the passage and answer the following questions.

Q: What do you notice for the first time? What stood out to you?

Q: What might this passage reveal to us about God or Jesus and his work or plans?

To stay in the spiritual infant or child stage, never maturing, is not an option. It is spiritual laziness. When spiritual children start to make disciples who make disciples, (even if one-step at a time), they move quickly into being a spiritual young adult who has overcome the evil one and is strong by abiding in God's Word (1 Jn 2:13–14). They transition quickly into a mature parent because they know Jesus and his plan for their life. This is evident in the spiritual maturity stages revealed in 1 John 2:13–14.

Matthew 28:19–20

"Therefore, go and make disciples of all nations, baptizing them in the name of the Father and of the Son and of the Holy Spirit, and teaching them to obey everything I have commanded you. And surely I am with you always, to the very end of the age."

The verb go means, as you go and the noun all nations does not necessarily mean nation states, but all people groups. Therefore, Jesus is saying to the disciples, go and make disciples as you go through everyday life, in your social and relational environments, with all kinds of people groups, at their home, at work, or walking along the road. As disciples of Christ, teaching them or telling them about Jesus' teaching or one of his stories from the Bible and baptizing them – being a part of introducing them to Jesus, where they can have a life changing experience with Jesus, and are converted into disciples who make other disciples. We need to raise up biblical disciples and send them into the world to all people groups, so they can raise up other disciples who grow into Christ-likeness.

Jesus' strategic approach was to create disciples who make other disciples by (*increasing oneself*), who move towards spiritual maturity. At maturity, spiritual parents, who care for spiritual infant and child believers, have the role of moving people towards spiritual maturity are (*increasing spiritual mature disciples for Christ*). Leaders who make other leaders, by training young adult believers towards future ministry leadership, are also (*increasing their ministry and other leaders*).

This Will Require Momentum

According to the dictionary, momentum is the motion of a moving body. Where there is momentum, something or someone is moving. This same process happens in our life as obedient disciples of Christ. A life changing experience with Jesus, the power of the Holy Spirit and a willingness to obey, calls disciples of Christ to act justly, to love mercy and to walk humbly with God (Mic 6:8). So, who are the people we are to act justly and to love mercifully? Zechariah 7:10 tells us to bring justice and mercy to those called the Quartet of the Vulnerable: the widow, the fatherless, the foreigner and the poor.

Today, we are surrounded by such people: widows, single parents, families with no present father, and migrants from other countries. Also, we live in a country that is spiritually poor, where many are blind and captives of sin and its slavery.

In Luke 4:18–19, Jesus read Isaiah 61:1 in the synagogue:

"The Spirit of the Lord is on me,
because he has anointed me

to proclaim good news to the poor.
He has sent me to proclaim freedom for the prisoners
and recovery of sight for the blind,

to set the oppressed free,
to proclaim the year of the Lord's favour."

We are called to share the good news of Christ to the lost and unengaged that will give sight to the blind and release prisoners from the darkness of slavery to sin. We are called to be there for the broken-hearted (Isa 61:1), showing Christ's grace and forgiveness to the widow, the fatherless, the foreigner, and the spiritually poor. We are called to live fearlessly and courageously, moving in the momentum of God's grace. The momentum of God's grace should move disciples along Jesus' increasing disciple making path as its main feature (Mt 28:19–20; Jn 13:15; 14:12; 17:4, 18; 20:21).

Walking Along the Increasing Features

- **INCREASING oneself, a follower of Christ**
  (Jn 17:4, 18; Mt 28:19–20; Acts 14:21).
  Disciples who make other disciples, helping people to trust and follow Jesus, who grow towards spiritual maturity.

- **INCREASING spiritually mature disciples for Christ**
  (Heb 5:11–6:2; Col 1:28).
  Spiritually mature disciples love and care for spiritual infants and spiritual children.

- **INCREASING volunteers for service** (Acts 2:45; 6:1–6).
  Church leaders train and teach disciples to serve or become involved in a church activity.

- **INCREASING seed sowers and harvest workers**
  (Lk 10:2; Mt 9:38).
  Church leaders train and teach disciples (in small groups), to move along the disciple making path. Small group leaders train and teach disciples (in small groups), for Storytelling Jesus' Story.

- **INCREASING leaders and one's ministry**
  (Jn 21:15–17; 1 Cor 15:7; Acts 9:1–31; 17:14–15).
  Leaders making leaders, training spiritual mature disciples towards future ministry shepherd leadership.

Application – For Now and in the Future

Spend 5 minutes in preparation for the application of this passage. Afterwards, share your answers with the group.

**Q: How are you going to increase yourself (Mt 28:18–20)
by moving from accumulating large numbers of people to
sending people out to make disciples who make other disciples
who move towards spiritual maturity?**

Q: Out of the three spiritual stages, where are you most at and how are you going to move forward? And how are you going to handle people at each stage?

Share to Win - Then Connect
Build to Move
Train to Send

Q: Are you moving in the momentum of God's grace? What does that look like for you?

Prayer

Lord, help us to move as we walk along the increasing disciple making path, and live out the examples you provided. We pray that you will give us an opportunity to share our discovery this week with someone as a part of attracting others to Christ or helping someone move towards spiritual maturity. Please help us to prepare and memorize the Bible passage and be ready to retell it on the date that has been allocated to us. For next week, help us Lord with all the preparation, invitations, the meal for next week. And please help our small group leader as he or she leads the discussion time after the story.

Preparation for the Next Study

Review and familiarize yourself with the increasing disciple making path. The first person Storytelling Jesus' Story needs to be ready. The small group leader needs to be ready for the decision time, see Leaders' Notes 7.

STORYTELLING JESUS' STORY

The Christmas Story: God has Moved into the Neighbourhood

God became human and moved into the neighbourhood, is the Christmas story of Jesus' conception, birth, and early childhood, along the chronological timeline of the following passages: Luke 1:26–38; Matthew 1:18–25; Luke 2:1–32, 39; Matthew 2:1–21 and Luke 2:40–52 (Thomas & Gundry, 1998, pp. 36-40).

Jesus is a real person, born into a real family, into a real place on earth, into a real time in history. Jesus is God, who came down to earth, became human and lived among us for a while. Simply stated, God moved into the neighbourhood to fix humanity's biggest problem, the sin and brokenness that Adam and Eve left behind. Let us have a look at how Jesus came into the world.

Now, this is how the birth of Jesus happened: God sent the angel Gabriel to Nazareth, a town in Galilee, to Mary who was engaged to wed Joseph, a descendant of David. The angel said to her, "Greetings, do not be afraid, Mary; God is going to bless you. You will conceive and give birth to a son, and you are to call him Jesus. He will do great things and will be called the Son of God. God will give him David's throne, and he will reign over his descendants forever and his kingdom will have no end."

Mary says, "Like, how is this going to happen, "since I am a virgin?"

The angel replied, "You will become pregnant through God's Spirit, so the holy one born will be called the Son of God, and no word from God will ever fail."

Mary answered, "I am the Lord's servant, if that's what he wants, so be it." Then the angel left her.

Mary became pregnant and Joseph found out, so the wedding was off, but because he loved her, he just wanted to dump her quietly.

That night, an angel of the Lord appeared to him in a dream and said, "Joseph descendant of David, do not be afraid to take Mary home as your wife, because what is conceived in her is from God's Spirit. She will give birth to a son, and you are to call him Jesus, because he has come to take away the sins of his people."

This was to fulfill what the Lord said through the prophet: "**The virgin will conceive and give birth to a son, and they will call him Immanuel**" [Isa 7:14], which means "God with us".

So, that is what Joseph did, he took Mary home as his wife. But he had no union with her until after she gave birth to Jesus.

The Birth of Jesus

In the days of Caesar Augustus, he issued a decree that a census take place of the entire Roman world. And everyone went to their own town to register.

Joseph was a descendant of David, so he went from Nazareth to Bethlehem, the city of David, to register with Mary, who was expecting a child. While they were there, Mary said to Joseph, "I'm having some contractions and my waters have broken" and she gave birth to Jesus and wrapped him in cloth and placed him in a manger, because there was no guest room for them in the Kataluma (the private inn).

The Shepherds

Now, shepherds were living out in the fields, watching their flocks at night. An angel of the Lord appeared to them, and said, "Do not be afraid. I bring you good news of great joy. Today in the city of David a Savior was born. You will find a baby covered in cloth and resting in a manger."

So, the shepherds set off for Bethlehem and found Mary and Joseph, and the baby, resting in the manger.

Jesus Presented in the Temple

On the eighth day, Mary and Joseph took Jesus to Jerusalem, to be circumcised, according to the Law of Moses. As it is written, **"Every firstborn male must be dedicated to God"** [Exod 13:2, 12], and make a sacrificial offering of **"a pair of doves or two pigeons"** [Lev 5:11; 12:8].

Now there was a man called Simeon. He had been told by God's Spirit that he would not die until he had seen the Lord's Chosen One. Simeon took Jesus in his arms and praised God, saying: **"My eyes have seen your salvation, which you have made for all humanity** [Isa 49:6], now I can die in peace."

When Joseph and Mary had done everything according to the Law of Moses, they returned to Galilee, to their own town of Nazareth.

The Move Back to Bethlehem

Approximately two years later, for some reason Mary and Joseph are back in Bethlehem, maybe they moved to Bethlehem to raise the Son of David in the city of David. Whatever the reason for moving, they are now living in a *"house"* (Mt 2:11) and Jesus had gone from being called a *"baby"* (Lk 2:6, 12, 16) to a *"child"* (Mt 2:9, 14), meaning Jesus is possibly around 2 years old (Cf. Mt 2:16).

The Magi Visit the Messiah

During the time of King Herod, Magi from the east came to Jerusalem and asked, "Can you tell us where is the one born king of the Jews? We saw his star when it rose and have come to worship him."

Upon hearing this King Herod was greatly disturbed, because he thought he was the King of the Jews. He called the religious leaders and asked them where the Chosen One would be born. "In Bethlehem," they answered, "because this is what the prophet has written: **"Out of Bethlehem will come a ruler, who will shepherd my people"** [Mic 5:2].

So, Herod got the Magi to tell him exactly when the star appeared. Then he told them the prophecy about Bethlehem, and said, "Go and look carefully for the child. As soon as you find him, report to me, so I may go and worship him as well."

So, the Magi went on their way. Then the star went ahead of them until it stopped over the place where the child was. When they arrived at the house, they saw the child with his parents, and they bowed down and worshipped him. Then they opened their treasures and presented him with gifts of gold, frankincense, and myrrh.[6] Yet, having been warned in a dream not to go back to Herod, they returned to their country by another route.

The Escape to Egypt

When they had gone, an angel of the Lord appeared to Joseph in a dream. "Get up, take the child and his mother and escape to Egypt. Stay there until I tell you, for Herod is going to search for the child to kill him."

So, he got up, took the child and his mother during the night, and left for Egypt, and stayed there until Herod died. This was to fulfill what the Lord had said through the prophet: **"Out of Egypt I called my son"** [Hos 11:1].

When Herod realized that the Magi had tricked him, he was furious, and he gave orders to kill all the boys in Bethlehem and its area who were two years old and under, according to the time the Magi had told him. This was to fulfill what the prophet Jeremiah said: **"Weeping and great mourning, Rachel weeping for her children and refusing to be comforted, because they are no more"** [Jer 31:15].

---

6 Frankincense is a fragrant tree sap resin from the *Boswellia* sacra tree, and it is used in perfume. Myrrh is a fragrant tree sap resin from the Commiphora myrrham tree, and it contains substances that could decrease pain and kill germs.

The Return to Nazareth

After Herod died, an angel of the Lord appeared in a dream to Joseph in Egypt, take the child and his mother and go to your land, because those who were trying to kill the child are dead."

So, they went back to Galilee and lived in a town called Nazareth. This was to fulfill what was said through the prophets, **that he would be called a Nazarene** [Ref. Ps 22:6–8, 13; 69:8, 20; Isa 11:1; 49:7; 53:2; 5, 8]. Jesus as a child grew up strong, wise, and God's favor was within him.

The Boy Jesus at the Temple

When Jesus was twelve years old, he went to Jerusalem for the Passover Festival with his parents. After the festival was over, while his parents were returning home, Jesus stayed behind in Jerusalem, but his parents were unaware of it, thinking he was with other relatives. When they did not find him, they went back to Jerusalem to look for him. They found him in the temple courts, with the teachers, listening to them and asking them questions. Everyone was amazed at his understanding and his answers. Mary said, "Your father and I have been worried to death about you."

He replied, "Why were you looking for me? Didn't you know I had to be in my Father's house?" But they did not understand what he was saying to them.

Then Jesus went back with his parents to Nazareth, and he obeyed them in everything, and he grew up strong, wise, and in favor with God and other people.

Discussion Questions

Q: In the story, what stood out to you for the first time?

Q: Alternative Question: Why would God bother moving into our neighbourhood?

Q: What did you learn in the story about God, Jesus and/or yourself?

Q: If this story is true and what you have learnt from it is true, how will you live differently because of what you have learned from it?

Devotion

The Christmas Story: God has Moved into the Neighborhood

ALONG THE CHRONOLOGICAL TIMELINE OF LUKE 1:26–38;
MATTHEW 1:18–25; LUKE 2:1–32, 39; MATTHEW 2:1–21 AND LUKE 2:40–52.

Jesus is the most significant person in all history, according to the New York Times (Faase, 2016, June 29). This would be because Jesus is God, who came down to earth, became human and lived together with us, some two thousand years ago. The word "Immanuel," means, *God is with us* (Mt 1:23), which is connected to Jesus moving *"into the neighborhood"* (Jn 1:14 MSG). The disciple John, as a witness stated, *"We saw the glory with our own eyes, the one-of-a-kind glory, like Father, like Son, generous inside and out, true from start to finish"* (Jn 1:14 MSG). Therefore, Jesus is absolutely 100% human and completely 100% God, simultaneously.

Jesus – Fact or Fiction

Jesus, is a real person, born into a real family (Joseph and Mary), born into a real place on earth (Bethlehem), into a real time in world history (late in the year of 6 B.C.), in the days of Caesar Augustus, while Quirinius was governor of Syria, and Herod the Great ruled over Israel for the Roman Empire. Jesus is God, the Saviour, the anointed Chosen One, Son of God and the forever King. Therefore, Jesus is the one invested with God's power to speak and act on his behalf. One's faith in Jesus is not based on a fairy tale story but is solidly anchored in actual history.

The Date of Jesus' Birth

The date of approx. 6 B.C. can be known as the day of Jesus' birth (Cox & Easley, 2007, p. 286), and others specify "late in the year of 6 B.C." (Thomas & Gundry 1998, p. 318).

Augustus was the Roman emperor between 30 B.C. to A.D. 14, and Quirinius was the governor of Syria between 8 B.C. to A.D. 6 (Thomas & Gundry 1998, p. 315). Therefore, the year of 6 B.C. does fit into the time of the census (Lk 2:1).

Herod the Great died in 4 B.C. and we know Jesus must have been born at least two years prior (Thomas & Gundry 1998, p 315). Therefore, the death of Herod remains the most certain reference pointing to Jesus' birth being around 6 B.C.

However, the main purpose of Luke's historical record is to show that Jesus was born in Bethlehem, the town of David (Mic 5:2), to fulfill where the chosen Messiah would be born (Schreiner, p. 807).

Seven Prophetic Fulfilment Statements

1. Jesus' Virgin birth (Isa 7:14; Cf. Gen 3:15;). Mary became pregnant through the Holy Spirit, so the holy one born would be called the Son of God, for nothing is impossible with God (Mt 1:20b; Lk 1:35, 37). This is how Jesus was fully human and fully God, at the same time. There is a song called, *"On My Father's Side"* (Unknown author, 2022, Apr 23), in which the words say, "On my mother's side (fully human) and on my Father's side (fully God)". Jesus' deity as the Son of God and his virgin birth lay behind this statement. Jesus' first recorded words was when he referred to God as *"my Father"* (Lk 2:49).

2. Simeon's salvation declaration, *"My eyes have seen your salvation, which you have made for all humanity"* [Isa 49:6], meant he could now die in peace (Lk 2:25–35). This is similar to Anna's testimony, who had been praying for the salvation of God's people (Lk 2:36–38).

3. Jesus was born in Bethlehem (Mic 5:2). Jesus' birth in Bethlehem, the city of David shows us the location where the chosen Messiah would be born, and who would become the shepherd leader to God's people.

4. Jesus is from David's royal family line (Lk 3:23–31). Jesus is a direct descendant of king David, as seen in Jesus' genealogy (Mt 1:1, 6–17). The royal line of Israel connects Jesus' humanity and qualifies him to be the chosen Messiah (Cox & Easley, 2007, p. 29).

5. *Out of Egypt I called my son* (Hos 11:1). Probably refers to Egypt's protection from the famine for Jacob's family and now Egypt offers protection to Jesus and his parents (Chamblin, p. 726).

6. *Rachel's weeping and mourning* (Jer 31:15). *Rachel weeps for her children and refusing to be comforted, because they are no more*, is seen as the lament for the mothers in Bethlehem. After Herod kills all the 2-year-old boys and under, which was seen as the massacre of all the male innocent children in that isolated area.

7. Jesus would be called a Nazarene, which probably refers to Jesus' humble beginning, and the rejection of the chosen Messiah (Ps 22:6–8, 13; 69:8, 20, 21; Isa 11:1; 49:7; 53:2, 5, 8).

Six Angelic Guidance's

1. The angel Gabriel said to Mary, *"You are going to give birth to a son"* (Lk 1:26).

2. The angel of the Lord told Joseph in a dream to take Mary as your wife (Mt 1:20).

3. The angel of the Lord appeared to the shepherds (Lk 2:9–12).

4. A great army of angels appeared to the shepherds (Lk 2:13–14).

5. The angel of the Lord told Joseph in a dream to flee to Egypt, for Herod wants to kill the child (Mt 2:13).

6. The angel of the Lord told Joseph in a dream in Egypt to move back to Israel (Mt 2:19–20).

The Distances They had to Travel

The distance between Nazareth and Bethlehem is 157 kilometres. Bethlehem to Jerusalem is 10 km. Jerusalem to Nazareth is 147 km. Bethlehem to Egypt is 700 km, and Egypt to Nazareth is 850 km. The Magi from the east (a faraway land) travelled an unknown distance. It took them two years to work out the star that rose in the east was about the birth of the King of the Jews (Mt 2:1-2), and then travel to Jerusalem.

There's No Guest Room in the Kataluma

In the birth scene, the word "*inn*" in the original Greek is *kataluma* (Lk 2:7), and the word "*inn*" in the Good Samaritan story is *pandokeion* (Lk 13:10–17). A *pandokeion* is a public inn where you paid for a room, whereas a *kataluma* is the spare room in a private home, which was free.

All Joseph had to say to a homeowner in Bethlehem was to state his genealogy back to King David and find out that they were distant cousins. This would give Joseph the right to free accommodation when travelling. But at that particular time, there was no guest room left, because of all the people coming to register for the census.

A normal home in Bethlehem, at that time, was a single room and the *kataluma* (the guest room) was on the side. Yet the stable was on the other side of the house. There was a window between the room and the stable, where food scraps were placed in the manger where animals could feed from. Mary was placed into a family home – the stable, where she would have had help in the birth from other women. Placing fresh straw onto the floor would be an exceptionally clean area for Mary to give birth to baby Jesus.

Who Witnessed Jesus' Birth?

Besides Joseph and Mary, Jesus' coming into the world was announced to poor shepherds in the open field (Lk 2:8–20), to the elderly, Simeon and Anna in the temple (Lk 2:22–38). Additionally, two years later the wealthy kings, the magi from a land far away (Mt 2:1–12), were the witnesses of the child Jesus.

The Emerging Question

Why is Jesus the most significant person in all history and why are his teachings so inground into today's society? It is because Jesus' teaching has deeply influenced Western society. For example – and to mention just a few – the notion of the equality of all people, helping and caring for the poor and marginalized, the dignity of women and children, education and medical care to be accessible to everyone, forgiveness to all people. The world we live in today is dramatically a better place because of Jesus, for these values did not exist before the time of Jesus (Faase, 2016, p. 1).

STORYTELLING JESUS' STORY

Jesus' First Followers:
Come, See and Follow Jesus

This story looks at Jesus' first followers, using the following passages to make a chronological timeline: John 1:35–46; Luke 5:1–11; Matthew 9:9–13 and Luke 6:12–16 (Thomas & Gundry, 1998, pp. 48, 57, 63–70). Will they come, see and follow him? Let's find out!

My name is John, and I am a fisherman and we have caught so many fish it is not funny. We have baked and shaken them. We have fried and dried them. We have salted and seasoned them. And there are still so many fish.

Well, let me tell you the story: A few months ago, at Bethany, along the Jordon River, John the Baptist was at his post with two disciples (Andrew and myself "John"). When he saw Jesus walking nearby, he said, "Look the Lamb of God, who takes away the sin of the world."

When the two of us heard this, we followed Jesus. Jesus looked over his shoulder and said to us, "What do you want?"

We said, "Teacher, where are you staying?"

He replied, "Come and see for yourself."

We came, saw where he was living, and ended up staying with him for the day. Andrew, and I "John" followed Jesus.

The first thing Andrew did was to find his brother, Peter, telling him, "We've found the Chosen One." Andrew immediately led him to Jesus. Jesus took one look and said, "You're Peter."

The next day Jesus went down to Galilee. When he got there, he ran into Philip and said, "Come, follow me." Philip found his friend Nathanael and told him, "We have found the One Moses, and the prophets wrote about. Jesus, from Nazareth!"

Nathanael said, "Nazareth? You have got to be kidding." But Philip said, "Come and see, come and check him out for yourself." When Nathanael saw Jesus, Nathanael declared "Teacher, I believe you really are the Son of God." Yet all of us did not follow Jesus permanently, at that time.

Sometime later, Jesus walked beside the Sea of Galilee the crowd were pushing in on him, to better hear the Word of God. Jesus saw boats tied up so he climbed into the boat belonging to Peter and asked him to push it out a little from the shore, so he could use Peter's boat as a platform to teach the crowd.

When he finished teaching, he said to Peter, "Push your boat out and let the nets out and catch some fish."

Peter said, "Teacher, we have been fishing all night and we caught nothing. But if you say so, I will let down the nets." And suddenly, a huge haul of fish, straining the nets to the point of breaking. Peter waved to his partners Andrew, James, and myself "John" in the other boat to come help. They filled both boats to the point where they were about to sink.

When Peter saw this, he fell to his knees before Jesus. "Teacher, go away, I am a broken man, and I can't handle this type of holiness". We were all overwhelmed by the number of fish that were caught.

Jesus said to Peter, "There is nothing to fear, follow me, and I will make you fish for people." They packed up their boats, left everything, and followed Jesus permanently.

As Jesus went on from there, he saw Matthew at his workplace collecting taxes. Jesus said to Matthew, "Come and follow me," and Matthew stood up and followed Jesus permanently.

Later when Jesus was having dinner at Matthew's house with his followers, a lot of dishonourable people came and joined them. When the religious leaders saw Jesus with these types of people, they had a fit, and said, "What kind of example is this from a teacher, acting cosy with crooks, and misfits?"

Jesus, overhearing them, said, "Who needs a doctor: the healthy or the sick? Go and learn what this means, **I want compassion, not religion** [Hos 6:6]. I am here to invite outsiders, not spoiled insiders."

Later, Jesus went up to a mountainside and spent the night praying before God. The next day, he called his disciples and from them he selected twelve: *Peter*, and his brother *Andrew*, (*James* and his brother *John*, the sons of Zebedee, who were also called the Sons of Thunder), *Philip*, *Nathanael*, who was also called Bartholomew, *Matthew*, *Thomas*, (*James*, the son of Alphaeus), *Simon* the Zealot, (*Judas* the son of James, who was also called Thaddaeus) and *Judas* Iscariot, who betrayed him.

This is the story of Jesus' first followers – *come*, *see*, and respond to Jesus' call to *follow* him. Will you do the same?

Discussion Questions

Q: In the story, what stood out to you for the first time?

Q: Alternative Question: Why would Jesus want people to follow Him?

Q: What did you learn in the story about God, Jesus and/or yourself?

Q: If this story is true and what you have learnt from it is true, how will you live differently because of what you have learned from it?

Devotion

Jesus' First Followers: Come, See and Follow Jesus

ALONG THE CHRONOLOGICAL TIMELINE OF JOHN 1:35–46; LUKE 5:1–11; MATTHEW 9:9–13 AND LUKE 6:12–16.

What is a Disciple?

The word disciple is the Greek word, *mathetes*, which means an active learner, actively learning to live like their teacher. This seems to be hard wired into all humanity because everyone follows something or someone and learns to live for or becomes like that person. However, Jesus said, *"No one can serve two masters"* (Mt 6:24). Every person on this earth has two choices. One is to follow and learn the ways of this world and its negative voices, therefore becoming a disciple of the Inner Critic, who drive or enslave people throughout their life (Thompson, 2019). The second choice is to respond appropriately to Jesus, by following Him, becoming his disciple, being built up by him, strengthened in their faith (Col 2:6), becoming like Christ (1 Jn 2:6; 1 Cor 11:1), by actively learning to live like Him. This choice shrinks and starves the Inner Critic and his negative voices (in Study 13 there will be more information on the Inner Critic).

A disciple moves and grows towards spiritual maturity because our goal is to present ourselves and other people as spiritually mature in Christ (1 Cor 14:20; Col 1:28; Heb 5:14; Jms 1:4). We achieve this by moving through five stages of spiritual growth.

Five Stages of Spiritual Growth

A disciple has ceased being *spiritually dead* in their brokenness (Eph 2:1–2) to being spiritually alive (Col 2:13). Therefore, becoming a *spiritual infant* (1 Pt 2:2). A new follower of Jesus finds repentance by turning back to God and dies to the network of lies that their lives once were built on, becoming *"reborn ...not [by] a physical birth ...but a birth that comes from God"* (Jn 1:3 NLT). Then a disciple grows from being a *spiritual infant* to a *spiritual child (1* Jn 2:12a, 14a), (Matthews, 2017), then to a *spiritual young adult (1* Jn 2:13b,14c) (Johnson, 1993, p. 50), and finally becomes a mature *spiritual parent (1* Jn 2:13a,14b, 1 Thess 2:11) (Akin, 2014, p. 37).

Why Do We Do This?

We do this to produce a disciple making movement. We want to create a movement of mature disciple makers, (increasing spiritual mature disciples for Christ). A disciple of Jesus is someone who follows Jesus at the head level, is being changed by Jesus at the heart level and is committed to the mission of Jesus at the hands on level (increasing oneself) as they accept the call to action. They live out a lifestyle of sentness. Some of these disciples become leaders who can make other leaders (increasing leaders and one's ministry). By doing this, some become coaches and others become peer supporters, to help care for spiritual infants and children, moving them towards maturity. This process follows a complex, linear progression from being spiritually dead, to becoming infants, then children, young adults next, and finally, mature parents. This is a vital process, as too many people stay in the *spiritually dead stage, unaware that they need to choose Jesus, to be spiritually reborn* (Jn 1:3 NLT). Also, *too many* Christians stay in the spiritual infant or child stage for years, never maturing (Heb 5:12–61a).

STORYTELLING JESUS' STORY

The Lost Animal, the Lost Money, and the Lost Son: Search and Rescue

This Study we are looking at Jesus' mission to search and rescue the lost and broken as seen in Luke 15:1–31. So far, following Jesus is about responding appropriately to him and actively learning from him. As the Christ (the Chosen One), Jesus possessed the power of God himself and was designated to search and rescue the lost and broken people. Let us have a look at how he did this!

Now the people were all gathering around to hear Jesus. But the religious leaders grumbled said, "What kind of teacher welcomes, eats and acts cozy with crooks, misfits, and tramps?"

So, Jesus told them this story. "Suppose one of you has one hundred animals and loses one. Don't you leave the ninety-nine and search for the lost animal and when you find it, you rescue it? And when you have rescued it, you joyfully put it on your shoulders as you go home. And then you call your friends and say, 'Rejoice with me; I have searched for and rescued my lost animal.' In the same way, there will be more rejoicing in heaven over one broken sinner who turns back to God than over the ninety-nine spoilt insiders, who do not think they need to turn back to God."

Suppose a woman has some housekeeping (let us say $1,000.00) and she loses it. Does she not search carefully until she finds it? And when she finds it, she calls her friends and says, 'Rejoice with me; I have searched for and found my lost money.' In the same way, there will be more rejoicing in heaven over one broken sinner who turns back to God."

Jesus continued: "There was a man who had two sons. The younger son said to his father, 'Father, give me my share of the estate.' So, he divided his property between them. When the younger son got everything, he set off for a distant country where he squandered his wealth in wild living. After he had spent everything, there was a severe famine in that whole country, and he began to be in need. So, he went and hired himself to feed pigs. He longed to eat what the pigs were eating, but no one gave him anything.

"When he came to his senses, he said, 'How many of my father's hired employees have food to spare, and here I am starving to death! I know what I will do, I will go back to my father and say, 'Father, I have turned away from heaven and against you. I am no longer worthy to be called your son: make me like one of your employees.' So, he got up and went back to his father.

"But while he was still a long way off, his father saw him and was filled with compassion for him; he ran to his son, threw his arms around him, and kissed him. The son said to him, 'Father, I have turned away from heaven and against you. I am no longer worthy to be called your son.'

"But the father said to one of his employees, 'Quick! Bring the best jacket and put it on him. Put a ring on his finger and shoes on his feet. Slaughter the fattened calf because we are having a BBQ feast.' For this son of mine was dead and is alive again; he was lost and has returned home. So, they began to celebrate.

"But the older brother grumbled, like the religious leaders, becoming angry and refusing to rejoice. Saying 'I have obeyed you in every way. But when this broken sinner, who squandered your resources, turns back to God the Father, you celebrate.'

"I tell you in the same way there will be more rejoicing in heaven with the angels over one broken sinner who turns back to God the Father, because they were dead and are alive again, they were lost, and have returned home."

Jesus' mission was to *search* for and *rescue* the lost, show them God's love and encourage them to return home for a whole new fresh start to their life. This is connecting God's story with our story.

Discussion Questions

Q: In the story, what stood out to you for the first time?

Q: Alternative Question: Why would Jesus want to search and rescue the lost?

Q: What did you learn in the story about God, Jesus and/or yourself?

Q: If this story is true and what you have learnt from it is true, how will you live differently because of what you have learned from it?

Devotion

The Lost Animal, the Lost Money, and the Lost Son:
Search and Rescue

LUKE 15:1–31.

Jesus the Rescuer

Following Jesus the Christ, the Chosen One (Lk 2:1–12, 26) is about responding appropriately to him and actively learning from Him. As Jesus possessed the power of God himself, he was designated to search out and rescue or save the lost and broken people (Lk 2:11). So, it is not surprising to see Jesus' mission as a rescuer.

But this raises two questions. Whom was Jesus to save? What was he to save them from? The answers have to do with God's consequence in the theme of divine judgement.

Jesus and Judgement

From Luke's gospel, you will have noticed that Jesus never shied away from addressing the theme of divine judgement (e.g., Lk 10:13–15; 11:31–32). As unpopular as this theme has become in modern society it is an unavoidable aspect of Jesus' message.

In fact, Jesus went as far as to say that, as the Christ, God had appointed him as the administrator of God's judgement. God's judgement is his way of displaying his love, mercy as well as his anger (2 Cor 5:10) (Youngblood, p. 590). In Luke 13:23, someone asks Jesus whether many will be saved from judgement. His response was fascinating.

Luke 13:22–30

Clearly, in Luke 13:26, the one who *"ate and drank ... and taught"* in the streets is Jesus himself. But he is also described as *"the owner of the house,"* that is, the one with authority to open or shut the door of God's kingdom on the people of the world.

On the one hand, it is comforting to know that someone as humble, just, and compassionate as Jesus is in charge of the judgement. But on the other hand, it is unnerving to know that this same Jesus was the one who was so outraged by hypocrisy, greed and injustice in all its forms. This passage should begin to make us wonder whether we will be among those welcomed into God's kingdom, so to speak, or locked out.

Jesus and the Rescue of Sinners

According to the opening verses in Luke 15:1–31, Jesus was again in trouble with the religious leaders for befriending *"men and women of questionable reputation"* (Lk 15:1 MSG), or *"sinners"* (Lk 15:1 NRSV), people that were broken, like a plate shattered in pieces on the ground. Most people understand that they and the world around them are broken. Some call this brokenness sin. The word, sinner, was a common way of referring to someone considered to be under God's judgment. Sin causes spiritual death but grace the free gift of God is eternal life in Christ Jesus (Rom 5:12; 6:23) (Harm, p. 1016).

The three stories in Luke chapter 15, explains why Jesus befriended broken sinners. The third story, the famous Prodigal Son, is particularly important. In it, Jesus offers both his own definition of a broken sinner and his own description of God.

Who is a Broken Sinner?

As we look closely at Luke 15:11–13, we see the younger son represents the broken sinner Jesus has been befriending. The older son represents the religious leaders, and the father represents God. The main offense of the younger man was not that he ended up in wild living, but rather using the father's resources and spending those resources on himself and living a great distance from the father, wanting all he could get from the father yet have nothing to do with him.

What is Brokenness or Sin?

How many could claim not to be broken sinners? Yet, many say, "I'm a good person, I'm not a murderer, theft or an adulterer." When comparing oneself to a criminal, you could come out looking pretty good. But when we compare ourselves to Jesus, the sinless person, we are all broken, we all fall short.

We, like the younger son, love to use God's resources of life, relationships, food, money, the environment and so on, but at the same time keep a distance from God himself, either by choice or neglect. We may not live wildly but we do live separately from the Father. According to Jesus, this is at the heart of brokenness and sin. Hardness of heart, unbelief, refusal to return to God and believe in his promises (Heb 3:8, 15; 4:7). A stubborn unwillingness to open ourselves to the love of God (2 Cor 36:13; Eph 4:18) and being insensitive to the needs of others (Deut 15:7; Eph 4:19), are also at the heart of brokenness and sin (Bloesch, p. 1012).

What is God like?

When we look closely at Luke 15:20–24, we find out that the father was looking out a window for the younger son and when he saw him while he is "*still a long way off*" (Jn 15:20). The father runs, embraces, and kisses the son even before his apology. No sooner does the son offer his apology than the father lavishes his gifts on the son and orders a great celebration. According to Jesus, God is a searching, running, embracing, pardoning, lavishing, partying parent.

God loves us and longs to receive us back. This is the reason Jesus befriended broken sinners. He wanted to assure them of God's love and convince them to come back to God. Turning back to God is where we get the word, "repentance", and we know forgiveness follows repentance.

Jesus was God's rescuer to search and find people who have distanced themselves from God and deserve his judgement and convince them to return home for a fresh start to their life.

The Emerging Question

Do we really want a fresh start to your life? Are we broken sinners who are still living at a distance from God? Or have we turned to him and sought his forgiveness?

STORYTELLING JESUS' STORY

Jesus, the Blind Man and Zacchaeus: Heal, Rescue and Restore

This study we're looking at Jesus' mission to heal, rescue and restore the lost, and broken, as seen in Luke 18:35-19:10. Parallel passages are Matthew 20:29-34 and Mark 10:46-52.

Jesus and his disciples are travelling on the road to the capital city of Jerusalem. In this story, they are approaching the city of Jericho, which is about 50 kilometres from Jerusalem. There they encounter two men from both ends of the socioeconomic spectrum. One is a poor blind beggar. The other is a wealthy tax officer. Let us look at this wonderful story!

As Jesus travelled towards the capital city, a blind man named Bartimaeus was sitting by the roadside begging. When he heard the crowd going by, he asked what was going on.

They told him, "Jesus of Nazareth is passing by." So, he called out, "Jesus, Son of David, have mercy on me!" The people told him off, and said to him "be quiet," but he shouted all the more louder, "Jesus, Son of David, have mercy on me!"

Jesus stopped and called the blind man. Throwing his jacket aside, he jumped to his feet and came to Jesus. Jesus asked him, "What do you want me to do for you?"

The blind man said, "Teacher, I want to see." Jesus touched his eyes and said, "Receive your sight; your faith has healed you." Immediately he could see and followed Jesus along the road, praising God. When all the people saw this, they too also praised God.

Jesus entered the next town, the town of Jericho. A man named Zacchaeus, a wealthy tax officer, wanted desperately to see Jesus, but because he was a short man, he could not see over the crowd. So, he ran ahead and climbed a sycamore-fig tree so he could see Jesus when he came by.

When Jesus reached the spot, he looked up and said, "Zacchaeus, come down immediately. Because I am coming to your house for tea." Zacchaeus was stoked about Jesus coming over for tea and could not get out of the tree quickly enough.

But all the people started to grumble, "What sort of a teacher acts cozy with misfits, crooks and thieving tax officers?"

But Zacchaeus stood up, a little stunned and said apologetically, "Teacher, I give half of my income to the poor and if I have cheated anybody, I'll pay them back four times the amount."

Jesus said to Zacchaeus in front of everyone, "Today this person has been rescued, because he too, is a part of God's family. Zacchaeus, you are free from the power your wealth had over you.

Jesus came to *rescue* and *restore* the fallen, the broken and bring them back into God's family. That is the result of fearless faith in Jesus. A person who is in God's family. You decide?

Discussion Questions

Q: In the story, what stood out to you for the first time?

Q: Alternative Question: Why would Jesus heal the blind man?

Or why would Jesus want to have dinner at Zacchaeus' house?

____

____

**Q: What did you learn in the story about God, Jesus and/or
yourself?**

____

____

**Q: If this story is true and what you have learnt from it is true, how
will you live differently because of what you have learned from it?**

____

____

Devotion

Jesus, the Blind Man and Zacchaeus:
Heal, Rescue and Restore

LUKE 18:35-19:10.

PARALLEL PASSAGES ARE MATTHEW 20:29-34 AND MARK 10:46-52.

So far, following Jesus is about responding appropriately to
him and actively learning from him. As the Chosen One, Jesus
possessed the power of God himself and was designated to search
and rescue the lost and broken people.

The Two Main People in the Story

Luke tells us, he is a blind man (Lk 18:35), and Mark tells us his
name – Bartimaeus, the son of Timaeus (Mk 10:46). Zacchaeus is
also named, and he is the chief tax collector for that area (Lk 19:1).

Socioeconomic Status

Bartimaeus is an extremely poor blind beggar and Zaccchaeus is
a wealthy tax collector. Zacchaeus later states he will *"give half of*
[his] *possessions to the poor"*(Lk 19:8). So, in that area, that should
balance the economy.

Both Men Wanted to See Jesus

The emphasis is on the word, "see", as Bartimaeus shouted, *"Jesus,*
Son of David, have mercy on me ... I want to see" (Lk 18:38–39,
41), and Zacchaeus wanted desperately to see Jesus (Lk 19:3).
They were both determined to attract the attention of Jesus, one
by shouting, the other by climbing a tree, in order to express
their faith in Jesus.

Jesus Has the Power to Heal

It is important not to see Jesus' healings merely as a party-trick or
proof of his power. They are actually signs of God's intention to one
day heal all the brokenness of our world and restoring the image of
God in humanity (Spiceland, p. 723). What Jesus did in history was a
kind of pledge to the reality that will exist in God's eternal kingdom.

Jesus' Two Titles

Jesus' title, "Son of David" is a Messianic title (meaning the Christ,
the anointed Chosen One). The blind man looked upon Jesus not
only as the one who could restore his sight (Isa 35:5), but also as
the one who would fulfil the promises made to King David (2 Sam
7:12 & 16; Ps 89:3–4; Isa 11:12; Jer 23:5–6; Ez 34;23–24; Jn 1:1–14)
(Thomas & Gundry, 1998, p. 166). The title, "Son of Man", is also a
Messianic title (meaning the Christ, God's anointed Chosen One),
and it appears eighty-two times in the gospels. It is the title Jesus
applies to himself, as he did in Luke 19:10: *"The Son of Man came*
to seek and to save what was lost".

Jesus' Right to be God's Spokesperson

Jesus is the Christ (the Messiah, God's Chosen one). This is the clarification of his identity as God's promised One, the person invested with God's authority to speak and act on God's behalf. Jesus is a clear and healthy voice amongst all the negative influential noise of the world (Spiceland, p. 723).

The Crowd's Response

The crowd praises God with Bartimaeus when his sight was restored (Lk 18:43). Yet the crowd is unhappy with Jesus when he announces he is going to Zacchaeus' house for a meal, saying, *"He has gone to be the guest of a sinner"* (Lk 19:7).

Jesus' Outreach

Jesus reached out to the tax collectors, or as the story states, he gets "cozy with crooks, misfits and thieving tax officers". In this instance, Jesus had visible fruit that Zacchaeus is freed from the power his wealth had over him (Lk 18:8–10).

In God's Family

The words, *"this person is a son of Abraham"* (Lk 19:9), not only refer to Zacchaeus' birthright to God's family, but also the birthright of those who believe in Jesus, who are born of God, who are children of God, and who belong in God's family (Jn 1:12–13). Being in God's family solves our identity and sin crises (Matthews, 2017).

The Emerging Question

Do we really want a fresh start to your life? Are we broken sinners who are still living at a distance from God? Or have we turned to him and sought his forgiveness?

STORYTELLING JESUS' STORY

Jesus Heals the Paralytic: Forgiveness

This study we are looking at Jesus' mission to heal and teach the people the good news of God's forgiveness as seen in Matthew 4:23–25 and Mark 2:1–12. Parallel passages are Matthew 9:1–8 and Luke 5:17–26.

The time has come to turn back to God, believe the good news and find eternal life. Jesus has the power and permission to forgive our sins. Even the spiritually paralyzed can find Jesus and have their failures, misdeeds, mistakes and transgressions forgiven. Let us have a closer look at this story.

Jesus traveled throughout the countryside, teaching in the religious places, telling everyone the good news of God's story and healing every disease and sickness among the people.

News about Jesus spread all over the place and people brought to him those who were poorly with various diseases, those suffering severe pain, the demon-possessed, those having seizures, and the paralyzed; and Jesus healed them all. Large crowds from all over the area followed Jesus.

When Jesus entered his hometown of Capernaum, the crowd gathered in such large numbers around his house that there was no room left, not even outside the door, as he taught God's word to them.

Four men carried their paralyzed friend on his mat and tried to take him into the house to place him before Jesus. When they could not find a way in because of the crowd, they went up onto the roof. They tied four ropes to the four corners of his mat, made an opening in the roof and then lowered the man into the middle of the crowd, right in front of Jesus.

When Jesus saw their faith, he said to the paralyzed man, "Friend, your failures, misdeeds, mistakes, and transgressions are forgiven."

Now some of the religious leaders, were saying to themselves, "Who does this guy think he is? Only God can forgive our transgressions."

Straightaway Jesus knew what they were thinking and asked, "Why are you thinking these evil things in your heart? Which is easier: to say to this paralyzed man, 'Your transgressions are forgiven,' or to say, 'Get up, pick your mat up and walk'? I will show you that I am the Son of Man, who has the power and permission to forgive our failures, misdeeds, mistakes, and transgressions." He said to the paralyzed man, "My man, get up, pick up your mat and go and walk home." Immediately the paralyzed man stood up in front of them, rolled up his mat and walked out in full view of them all.

Everyone saw this and was filled with awe. This is amazing and everyone started to praise God, saying, "We have never seen anything like this! Today, we have seen something extraordinary."

Today, even the spiritually paralyzed can find Jesus and have their failures, misdeeds, mistakes, and transgressions forgiven. So, why not get up and walk to Him! You have nothing to lose.

Discussion Questions

Q: In the story, what stood out to you for the first time?

Q: Alternative Question: Why would Jesus forgive the paralysed man?

Q: What did you learn in the story about God, Jesus and/or yourself?

Q: If this story is true and what you have learnt from it is true, how will you live differently because of what you have learned from it?

Devotion

Jesus Heals the Paralytic: Forgiveness

MATTHEW 4:23–25 AND MARK 2:1–12.
PARALLEL PASSAGES ARE MATTHEW 9:1–8 AND LUKE 5:17–26.

The reason why Matthew 4:23-25 has been placed with the story "Jesus heals the paralytic". Because it is a great introduction into this story, the last illness described in Matthew 4:23 is "paralysed", which connects well into Jesus heals the paralytic.

So far, following Jesus is about responding appropriately to Jesus and actively learning from Him. As the Christ, Jesus possessed the power of God himself. Jesus' mission was to search and rescue the lost and heal the broken.

Jesus' Threefold Power for Ministry

The threefold power of Jesus' ministry was to teach in Jewish synagogues, proclaim (declare or tell) the good news of the kingdom of God, and heal diseases and sicknesses (Mt 4:23) in declaration of his authority to teach and preach the people (Thomas & Gundry, 1998, p. 60).

Jesus Taught in Jewish Synagogues

It is the same strategy Paul and the apostles used as they spread the gospel. They started with their own people, the Jews.

Jesus Told Everyone the Good News

Proclaiming the good news (the gospel of Jesus) can also be stated as, telling people about Jesus' story. The essence of Jesus' story is "*come follow Jesus*" (Mk 1:17), come close to Jesus and observe more carefully how to be like him, by first turning back to God, which is repentance, finding eternal life. It is the same message as in Mark 1:14, "*Jesus proclaimed the good news of God. The time has come; the kingdom of God has come near. Repent and believe the good news!*"

Jesus Healed Diseases and Sicknesses

People brought to Jesus those who were ill with various diseases, those suffering severe pain, the demon-possessed, those having seizures, and the paralysed and Jesus healed them (Mt 4:24).

Capernaum Jesus' Hometown

Jesus makes the physical move from the small town of Nazareth to the more populated city of Capernaum (Mt 4:13). Some believe Joseph has passed away. Jesus, the oldest son, becomes the head of the house and moves his mother and his siblings with him. The move to Capernaum also fulfils Isaiah's prophecy, "[The] *land of Zebulun and the land of Naphtali... in the future, he* [Jesus] *will honour Galilee... by the Way of the Sea, beyond the Jordan*" (Isa 9:1; Mt 4:15–16). Capernaum became Jesus' new home after his unfriendly reception at Nazareth (Lk 4:16–31) (Thomas & Gundry, 1998, p. 56). At that time, Capernaum had become a large city, with a tax office (Mt 9:9) and a garrison of Roman soldiers (Mt 8:9). Jesus taught in the city's synagogue, which had been built by the good centurion (Lk 7:5) and where Jairus was an official (Mk 5:22).

The Religious Leaders

They came from every village in the regions of Galilee and Judea and from Jerusalem. Some of the religious leaders seemed dead set on proving that Jesus was not God. But they had their hopes crushed as God the Father sent four incredible friends, who would not be denied, nor would they give up. Instead, they got creative in doing whatever it took to get their paralysed friend to Jesus (Edwards, 2010, p. 100).

Notice How They Leave This Outreach Event

They all (including the religious leaders) saw what happened and were struck with awe. It is amazing how they praised God: "We have never seen anything like this! Today, we have seen something extraordinary."

Forgiveness

Jesus the Son of Man has the power and permission to forgive our sins. To forgive all our failures, misdeeds, mistakes and everything we have done wrong. Remember, the essence of sin is using God's resources of life such as relationships, food, money, the environment and so on, but at the same time keeping a distance from God. Forgiveness is found when we turn back to God, living close to Him, yet still enjoying all his resources. Forgiveness is a basic human longing. Even the spiritually paralysed can find Jesus and have their failures, misdeeds, mistakes and transgressions forgiven.

The Emerging Question

Are you broken by your failures, misdeeds, mistakes and transgressions. Are you fed up with living at a distance from God? Are you willing to turn back to Jesus and sought his forgiveness? You ready can find a fresh start to your life. Your choice!

STORYTELLING JESUS' STORY

Jesus Calms the Storm and Heals the Demonic: Heals and Restores

This study we're looking at how Jesus has the power to control the environment as seen in Luke 8:22–39. Parallel passages are Matthew 8:18, 23–27 and Mark 4:35–41.

Not only does Jesus have the power to control the environment, but he can overcome evil, heal, and forgive people's brokenness and transgressions. Let me tell you the story!

After a long day of doing acts of kindness and teaching the crowds of people, Jesus said to his disciples, "Let us go over the other side of the lake." So, they got into a boat and set out. As they sailed, Jesus curled up with a pillow, absolutely exhausted and fell asleep at the rear of the boat.

Later a furious storm came down on the lake, where the wind, the rain and the waves started to swamp the boat, and they were in great danger. The disciples woke Jesus up, saying, "Teacher, don't you care, we're all going to drown!"

Jesus got up and said to the wind, the rain and the waves, Be Quiet! And immediately the wind, the rain and the waves were still. Jesus said to his disciples, "Where's your faith in me?"

In fear and astonishment, they asked each other, "Who is this guy? Even the wind, the rain and the waves obey him."

Jesus Restores a Demon-Possessed Man

They sailed to the region of Decapolis, the other side of the lake from Galilee. When Jesus stepped ashore, he was met by a demon-possessed man from the town. For a long time, this man had not worn clothes and was living in the cemetery, in a solitary place, screaming all night long. The town folk tried to chain him to a tombstone, but he broke the chains, and the town folk were very afraid of him.

When he saw Jesus, he cried out and fell at his feet, shouting at the top of his voice, "What do you want with us, Jesus, Son of the Most High God? We beg you, do not torture us or order us to go into the Abyss!" Because Jesus had commanded the impure spirit to come out of the man.

A large herd of pigs was feeding on the hillside. The demons begged Jesus to let them go into the pigs, and he gave them permission. When the demons came out of the man, they went into the pigs, and the herd ran down the hill into the lake and drowned.

When those tending the pigs ran off and reported this to the town folk, and the people came out to see what had happened. When they came to Jesus, they found the man who had been demon possessed, sitting at Jesus' feet, dressed and in his right mind. So, the pig herders told the people how the demon-possessed man had been cured. Then all the people of the region of Decapolis asked Jesus to leave.

The healed man asked if he could go with Jesus, but Jesus said, "No, return home to your family and your community and tell everyone how much God has done for you." Jesus got into the boat and left.

In fact, Jesus came through the region of Decapolis three months later and the people receive Jesus well (Mk 7:31–36). This had to be because the healed man had told everyone about what Jesus did for him. The man who was demon possessed but now in his right mind, prepared the way for Jesus' return a few months later. That is the power of fearless faith in Jesus, a person who was healed and restored by Jesus, but you decide.

Jesus calls us to believe and follow him, become one of his disciples, followers who actively learn to be like Jesus. So, what have you got to lose?

Discussion Questions

Q: In the story, what stood out to you for the first time?

Extra Discussion Questions

(See Leaders' Notes 11)

Q: In what other ways does Jesus control the environment?

Q: What do you think about the idea that evil tried to stop Jesus coming to Decapolis (a predominant Gentile region)? Therefore, who starts storms (God or the devil)?

Q: If a person is not for Jesus, by default, they are serving the Inner-Critic (the devil), which might be some form of evil possession, or they live in fear of evil spirits (hearts are hard and their ears don't want to hear, because of the Inner-Critic). So how much influence does the Inner-Critic have on the average Christian?

Q: Why would Jesus forbid some people to speak about being cured or healed, yet in this situation he said, "Go tell everyone"?

Q: If this story is true and what you have learnt from it is true, how will you live differently because of what you have learned from it?

Devotion

Jesus Calms the Storm and Heals the Demonic:
Heals and Restores

LUKE 8:22–39. PARALLEL PASSAGES ARE MATTHEW 8:18, 23–27 AND MARK 4:35–41.

Jesus Has the Power to Control the Environment

Life can sometimes be dangerous. In a small boat crossing the Sea of Galilee, suddenly a furious storm came down on the lake *"so that the boat was being swamped"* (Lk 8:23). It is no wonder that the disciples felt *"they were in great danger"* (Lk 8:23). Jesus has the power to not only stop the rain and wind, but he also immediately calmed the waters. Ordinarily, the waters would remain rough for a time after the wind stopped, but not this time.

Have you had any storms in your life? Jesus the Mighty Warrior is waiting for you to come to the end of yourself and start depending on Him. Practice saying, "Jesus, save the day" during the storms in your life. *"The Lord your God is with you, the Mighty Warrior who saves. He will take great delight in you; in his love he will no longer rebuke you but will rejoice over you with singing"* (Zeph 3:17).

Jesus Has the Power to Overcome Evil

Today, a sizeable portion of the human population does not recognize Jesus as the Most High God, but the demons do, and they are not going to heaven (Lk 8:28). In fact, the demons fully know that one day they will be tormented in the abyss of hell (Lk 8:31). The demons' master, the devil, dreads to be unclothed and would prefer to be in the pigs than in the abyss.

Jesus Has the Power to Heal and Restore People

Jesus drove out the evil spirits or "Legion", meaning many demons (Mk 5:9) from the man. Yet, Matthew states there were two demon-possessed men (Mt 8:28), but Mark and Luke single out the one who was the leader. These evil spirits had seized him many times, had tormented him and driven him to live naked in the cemetery, a solitary place, away from his family and his community (Lk 8:27–29). Jesus healed and restored the man who was demon possessed, so he was now *"dressed and in his right mind"* (Lk 8:35b). He can do the same today.

Jesus Has the Right to Question our Faith, in Difficult Times

The disciples were still struggling with their faith in Jesus, in the fearful storm, asking if their teacher cared that they might drown (Mk 4:38b)? After Jesus calmed the storm, the disciples wondered, *"Who is this [guy]? Even the winds and the waters obey him"* (Lk 8:25b). Even the privileged insiders still needed much strengthening in conviction about Jesus' identity. The people of that region were struggling with Jesus because of the death of their pigs. They asked Jesus to leave them because they were overcome with fear (Lk 8:37). Yet the man who had been demon possessed but was now in his right mind, has so much faith in Jesus he wants to go with him. But Jesus tells him to return home and tell his family and the people in his community, how much God has done for him, which he did (Lk 8:38–39).

Jesus comes through that region of Decapolis three months later and the people receive Jesus well (Mk 7:31–36). This had to be because the healed man had told everyone about what Jesus did for him. The man who was demon possessed but now in his right mind, prepared the way for Jesus' return a few months later (Thomas & Gundry, 1998, p. 93). That is the power of fearless faith in a person who was healed and restored by Jesus.

Shrink or Starve the Inner Critic

Throughout one's life, the Inner Critic has been changing the neural pathways in our brain, which changes our behavior. Negative words spoken to us or our bad experiences or worldly influences lodge negative thoughts into our mind, where he says, "You are stupid, dumb, immature, fat, thin, ugly, horrible, you don't need God, ect". Even though we might have had many good things said to us or good things happen to us, we often focus on the negative. Negative feelings drive our life: our behavior, our anger, anxiety, feelings of worthlessness, worry or fear (Thompson, 2019). And the Inner Critic is laughing in the background.

Throughout the stories of Jesus calming the storm and healing the demonic (Lk 8:22–39), fear stands out. The disciples were afraid of the storm (Lk 8:24, 25). The people of the town were afraid of Jesus who cured the demon-possessed man (Lk 8:35). They asked Jesus to leave the region because they were overcome with fear (Lk 8:37). In this passage, can you see any other behaviors that drive anger, anxiety, feeling down or worry?

The negative influence of the Inner Critic are lies that distort our thoughts, beliefs, feelings and free will. Therefore, the Inner Critic needs to be confronted when we acknowledge that such things are lies and distortions. One way of overcoming such issues is to write and speak out loud true statements frequently. The positive effect of this practice automatically changes the neural pathways which change our behavior. This is a God given ability to transform our mind, as Romans 12:2 states: *"Be transformed by the renewing of your mind."*

Write and Speak Out Loud These Truths, 5 or 6 Times

- People in general (or someone specific) have said bad things and hurt me.
- These people are human. They are not perfect, and they make mistakes just like everybody else.
- When I came to this place (home, workplace, church, etc.), no one gave these people a book on how to treat me.
- This stuff does not belong to me, and it is not good for me or anyone else.
- My family loves me very much and they want the very best for me.
- Because of all of this, I have now made a decision, to let all of the anger, anxiety, feeling down, worry or fear go (Ps 55:22; 1 Pt 5:7).
- Because of all of this, I have now made a decision to brush off all of the stuff that does not belong to me (the anger, anxiety, feeling down, worry or fear). (Use a brushing action, as if brushing something off your arm, waist and legs).

This works because these WORDS are true, and the truth will set you free (Jn 8:32). If they are not working all that good, repeat these true WORD statements, another five to six times. Also, repeat these true WORD statements whenever anger, anxiety, feeling down, worry or fear arises (Thompson, 2019).

Note: You may not be able to fully remove these nasty emotions, because they are a part of your personality. And it could take approximately three to four months to feel in control of these emotions. It's the control we are looking for, *"be angry, but don't sin"* (Eph 2:26). It's OK to be angry, but to have control is a wonderful thing. I personally have been placed into some horrible situations, where I could have easily lost it (became angry). But as I have driven home, I have even surprised myself, I didn't get angry.

Remember, these *TRUE WORDS* build up a defence that *shrinks* and *starves* the Inner Critic, because his destiny is getting hotter and ending closer every day.

(See Leaders' Notes 12)

The Emerging Question

Do we really want a fresh start to your life? Are we broken sinners who are still living at a distance from God? Or have we turned to him and sought his forgiveness?

STORYTELLING JESUS' STORY

Jesus Heals the Woman Hemorrhaging for 12 years: Your Faith Has Made You Well

This study we are looking at how Jesus has the power to make people well as seen in Mark 5:21 and 24–34. Parallel passages are Matthew 9:20–22 and Luke 8:40 and 42b–48.

In this story, this woman learnt the secret of tapping into Jesus' healing power. Well, let's have a look and see what happens.

Jesus crossed over by boat, from Decapolis to the other side of the lake, his hometown of Capernaum, where a large crowd welcomed him at the shoreline. The whole crowd were pushing, shoving and pressing around him.

There was a woman who had suffered from hemorrhaging for twelve years. She had suffered a long time under the care of many doctors, who could not heal her, had taken all her money and left her worse off than before. When she heard that Jesus was nearby, she snuck behind him and touched his garment.

She was thinking to herself, "If I can touch his clothes, I can get well." The moment she touched his garment, immediately the bleeding stopped. She could feel the change in her body, and she was finally freed from her suffering.

At the same moment, Jesus realized that power had gone out of him. He turned around to the crowd and asked, "Who touched my clothes?" When they all denied it, one of his disciples said, "What are you talking about? The crowd has been pushing and shoving around you, and you are asking, 'Who touched me?' Dozens of people have touched you!" But Jesus insisted "Someone touched me; I know that power has gone out of me," as he was still looking around to see who had done it.

The woman, knowing she was the one, frightened and trembling, stepped forward and said, "It was me." And in front of all the people she blurted out her story. "I have been hemorrhaging for twelve years, under the care of many doctors who could not heal me, took all my money and left me worse off than I was before. I thought, 'If I can touch your clothes, I will get well.' And that is why I touched you and the moment I touched you; I was healed."

Jesus said to her, "Be encouraged, your faith has healed you. Go in peace and be free from your suffering."

Jesus have compassion for blind and paralysed men, who were touched by him, to heal them. He also has compassion for women, who reach out to him, and believe that to touch his clothes would heal them. Because real faith in Jesus, is believing you can reach out to him, finding his arm stretched out to you. Hey! It's your choice.

Discussion Questions

Q: In the story, what stood out to you for the first time?

Q: In this story, what is the main idea?

Q: What did you learn in the story about God, Jesus and/or yourself?

Devotion

Jesus Heals the Woman Hemorrhaging for 12 years:
Your Faith Has Made You Well

MARK 5:21, 24–34.
PARALLEL PASSAGES ARE MATTHEW 9:20–22 AND LUKE 8:42B–48.

So far, following Jesus is about responding appropriately to him
and actively learning from Him. As the Christ, the anointed Chosen
One, Jesus possessed the power of God himself. Jesus has the power
to control the environment and to overcome evil. Jesus' mission was
to search and rescue the lost, heal the broken, provide forgiveness to
those who turn back to God and follow Jesus, becoming his disciples,
followers who actively learn to live like Jesus did.

Capernaum is Jesus' Hometown

Jesus is living in the city of Capernaum (Mt 4:13) and he has
established his headquarters there, which is a central area for Jesus
to move around as a travelling Teacher. Mark 5:20 shows us that
Jesus was in Decapolis and *Jesus* has *"crossed over by boat to the other
side of the lake"* (Mk 5:21) to Capernaum, as seen in the reference
to Jairus, who was the synagogue leader at Capernaum (Mk 5:22).

How Were Women Seen Back Then?

In the Greco-Roman world, women were seen as inferior to men,
not on the same level. Jewish men would regularly thank God in

prayer that they were not a Gentile, a slave or a woman (Faase, 2016, p. 36). However, throughout Jesus' teaching he was deeply inclusive of women. Jesus went out of his way to give women a sense of worth. In early Church history in the Greco-Roman world, Christian women experienced more freedom than usual in that culture (Faase, 2016, p. 31).

Jo Vitale has described how she feels in the church: "I have found a freedom that I do not see anywhere else in our culture. A freedom from being objectified, from being seen as just a sexual object, a freedom to become who God has called me to be in every aspect of life, and it is not about meeting cultural expectations and what society says I have to do. Actually, it is about who God calls me to be" (Faase, 2017, June 9).

Jesus' teaching has deeply influenced Western society. For example, our values of equality of all, caring for the poor and marginalized, the dignity of women and children, and forgiveness, to name a few. Yet, I believe, there is a lot more to be accomplished to protect, respect and value women. To follow Jesus' teaching will end inequality for women within our culture.

Jesus Has the Power to Heal

The power that had gone out from Jesus is the incredible healing power that comes from the Holy Spirit (Mk 5:30). Jesus began his ministry in *"the power of the Spirit"* (Lk 4:14) and *"the Spirit of the Lord"* allowed his ministry *"to release the captives and* [recover sight] *for the blind, to let the oppressed go free"* (Lk 4:18 NRSV). Remember this is not a party-trick or proof of his power. They are signs of God's intention one day to heal all the brokenness of our world. What Jesus did in history was a kind of pledge to the reality that will exist in God's eternal kingdom.

The Woman in the Story

Jesus' reservoir of power is always full, so he knew that *"power had gone out from [him]"* (Mk 3:30 NRSV). Yet this woman learnt the secret of tapping into it. She told Jesus why she touched his clothes and how she had been immediately healed from twelve long years of suffering. Note Jesus' response, *"Daughter, your faith has made you well. Go in peace and be freed from your suffering"* (Mk 5:34b NRSV).

Previous Healings

Jesus had compassion for blind and paralysed men (Lk 18:35–43 and Mk 2:1–12) who got Jesus' attention by shouting out loud or being lowered from the roof. Jesus also had compassion for women, who quietly reached out to him, believing that touching his clothes would make them well.

We also can find faith in Jesus, when we reach out to him anytime and find his arm stretched out to you.

The Emerging Question

Will you reach out to Jesus to find his arm stretched out to you? Go on and try it, you will see!

STORYTELLING JESUS' STORY

Jesus is the Only Trustworthy
Path to Heaven

This study we are looking at how Jesus is the only trustworthy path to heaven as seen in John 14:1–15. Jesus had a plan that would spread to about 56 percent of the Roman Empire – that's about 34 million Christian believers – around the mid fourth century. Throughout the centuries Christianity has become a global faith that surpasses cultures, social classes, languages and ethnic people groups (Stark, 1996, p. 7). Let us have a look at how he started this!

Jesus said, "Do not let this rattle you. Believe in God, believe in me also. In heaven, there are countless rooms in my father's house. I am about to hit the road along the path back to God the Father, to get your rooms ready. So, if I go and get your rooms ready, I will be back to get you, so you can live where I live. You already know the way along the path I am going."

Thomas said, "We have no idea where you are going. How do you expect us to know the way along the path?"

Jesus said, "I am the path to the reality of eternal life." It is the same as Jesus is the way, the truth, and the life. No one can return back to God, except through Jesus. If you really knew me, you would know God as well. From now on, you do know God. Because you have seen me!"

Philip said, "Show us God and it will gratefully satisfy us."

Jesus replied, "Philip, you have been with me all this time, and you still don't understand me? To see me is to see God. So how can you ask, 'Show us God.' Don't you believe that I am in God and He is in me? These words I am saying, I have not made up. They are from God the Father, who lives in me, who is doing his work.

"Believe me: I am in God and God is in me. If you cannot believe that, believe in the works I have done. The blind see, the lame walk, the deaf hear, the dead are raised, and the poor have learnt that God is on their side. The person who believes me will not only do what I have been doing but even greater things, because I am on the path to heaven, returning back home to God, and I am giving you the same work to do that I have been doing. I really mean it, whatever you ask in my name, I will do it.

Jesus is about to hit the path to heaven, to return back home to God the Father. There is no other path to heaven except through Jesus. If you love Jesus, you will treasure his instructions.

Jesus' disciple making path is about connecting your life story to Jesus' story, which will give you a better end to your life story, forever. Do you want a better ending to your life story? If the answer is "Yes". Well, it is through Jesus. So, what have you got to lose?

Discussion Questions

Q: In the story, what stood out to you for the first time?

Q: In this story, what is the main idea?

Q: What did you learn in the story about God, Jesus and/or yourself?

Devotion

Jesus is the Only Trustworthy Path to Heaven

JOHN 14:1–15.

Jesus told his disciples again that he is about to leave them but not to be afraid, because he is leaving them to prepare a place in heaven for them. He reminds them that he is the path to heaven (Jn 14:6). Jesus is about to hit the path to the trustworthiness of eternal life, back home with God the Father, in heaven.

Jesus the Way, the Truth and the Life

If you are on the path to the reality of eternal life, you know where you have been, and you know where the destination is. Jesus was born, lived his life through the truth of his teaching, died, rose from the dead and ascended to heaven. The way to heaven is the way Jesus paved along the path. The truth of heaven is through Jesus because he rose first. Jesus' resurrection guarantees our place, for those who have placed their faith in Him. It is true, you really can have a better end to your life story, both here on earth and forever in heaven.

Our Relationship with Jesus

Jesus is leaving but he is not leaving his disciples alone. Jesus left the Holy Spirit to be in their lives. Jesus promised to leave a friend the Spirit of Truth (Jn 14:15), a comforter, who would never leave. The Holy Spirit will live with us and will be in us (Jn 14:17). He will make his home in us (Jn 14:23), as he teaches us all sorts of things and reminds us of the things we have already learnt (Jn 14:26). Our relationship with Jesus is forever eternally linked to God the Father and the Holy Spirit.

Doing the Works That I do

If we are on the path to the reality of eternal life, we will know the works that Jesus did, and we will do the same. In fact, we will do greater works (Jn 14:12). The disciple making path is the work Jesus was talking about, disciples who make disciples, who make disciples, moving people towards spiritual maturity (as seen in study 1), along the directional moves from *share to win*, then *connect, build to move*, then *train to send*, as described in studies 2 to 7.

If We Love Jesus, We Will Treasure His Teachings

Jesus' greatest teachings is to love God and love people (Mt 22:36–40). All the teachings from the Bible hang on these two, love God and love others. These are the first and second greatest instructions ever give to humanity. Walking and working along the disciple making path, moving people towards spiritual maturity is a great way to treasure his teachings.

The Emerging Question

Will you love God and love other people as you connect your story to Jesus' story, which will give you a better end to your life story, forever? Then will you help connect others to Jesus' story, who go on connecting other people to Jesus' story, so we all can have a better end to our life stories? Will you walk along the disciple making path laid out for your life and for Jesus' mission? (Mt 28:19–20; Jn 13:15; 14:12; 17:4, 18; 20:21; Eph 3:10–11).

STORYTELLING JESUS' STORY

The Easter Story: Jesus' Crucifixion, Death, Burial, and Resurrection

In this study we are about to hear the Easter story, the story of Jesus' crucifixion, death, burial, and resurrection, along the chronological timeline of Matthew 27:31–61; Luke 23:55–56; Matthew 27:62–66; John 20:1–29; 1 Corinthians 15:6; John 20:30–31. Let us have a look at this beautiful story!

With trumped up charges they arrested Jesus, the perfect man, beat him and led him away to be crucified. They led him to a place called "The skull", where the soldiers nailed Jesus' hands and feet to the cross. Jesus was crucified between two other men, one on his right and one on his left.

The Roman cross was a brutal way of executing a person. Not only was it a way for everyone passing by to mock or hurl insults. But also, every time the person wanted to breathe in, they had to push their feet up on the nail, in agony, to do so. Subsequently, the cross was an execution of suffocation.

The Death of Jesus

From noon until three in the afternoon, darkness came over the land. As all our brokenness and sin was placed onto Jesus and he took them away, as he paid the price for our forgiveness [1 Cor 15:3; Col 2:13–14]. About three in the afternoon an earthquake shook the area as Jesus cried out in a loud voice, "The debt has been paid, and it is finished", and Jesus gave up his spirit and died.

Watching from a distance was John and a few women. Among the women were Mary Magdalene, Jesus' mother, and James and John's mother.

The Burial of Jesus

As evening approached, a rich man named Joseph, a disciple of Jesus went to Pilate, asking for Jesus' body. Pilate ordered that it be given to him. Joseph took the body, wrapped it in a clean linen cloth, and placed Jesus in a new tomb that he had cut out of the rock for himself. He rolled a huge stone in front of the entrance to the tomb and then he went away.

Mary Magdalene and some of the other women, who came with Joseph, sat opposite the tomb. Later they went home too.

The Guard at the Tomb

The next day, the religious leaders went to Pilate, and said, "we remember that Jesus said, 'After three days I will rise again.' So, give the order for the tomb to be made secure until the third day. Otherwise, his disciples may come and steal the body and tell the people that he has been raised from the dead. Pilate answered, "Take a guard, go, make the tomb secure. Place a seal on the stone and post the guard."

The Resurrection

Early on Sunday the first day of the week, while it was still dark, Mary Magdalene went to the tomb and saw that the stone had been removed from the entrance and Jesus' body was not in the tomb. So, she came running to Peter and John and said, "They have taken the Lord out of the tomb, and we don't know where they have put him!" So, Peter and John ran to the tomb, to find only the strips of linen lying there. John said, "He believed." Yet, they still did not understand from Scripture that Jesus had to rise from the dead. Then the disciples went back to where they were staying.

Jesus Appears to Mary Magdalene

Now Mary stood outside the tomb crying. As she wept, she looked into the tomb and saw two angels in white, seated where Jesus' body had been. They asked her, "Ma'am, why are you crying?" She said, "They have taken my Lord away, and I don't know where they have put him." At this, she turned around and saw Jesus standing there, but did not realize that he was Jesus. He asked her, "Ma'am, why are you crying? Thinking he was the gardener, she said, "Sir, if you have carried him away, tell me where you have put him, and I will get him." Jesus said to her, "Mary." She turned toward him and cried out, "Teacher!" But Jesus said, "Do not hold on to me, for I have not yet returned to the Father. Go to my brothers and tell them, I have risen." Mary Magdalene ran to the disciples with the news: "I have seen the Lord!" And told them what he had said.

Jesus Appears to His Disciples

On Sunday evening, when the disciples were together, with the doors locked in fear of the religious leaders, Jesus came and stood among them and said, "God's peace be with you!" He showed them his hands. The disciples were overjoyed when they saw him. Jesus said, "God's peace be with you! As the Father has sent me, I am sending you." And he breathed on them and said, "Receive God's Spirit. "Go and forgive as I have forgiven you," do acts of kindness and heal the sick [Mk 16:18b].

Jesus Appears to Thomas

Now Thomas, one of the twelve, was not with the disciples at that particular time. So, the other disciples told him, "We have seen Jesus!" But he would not believe, saying, "Unless I see the nail marks in his hands and put my finger where the nails were, I will not believe."

A week later the disciples were in the house again, and Thomas was with them. Though the doors were locked, Jesus came and stood among them and said, "God's peace be with you!" Then he said to Thomas, "Put your finger here in my hands. Stop doubting and believe."

Thomas said to him, "My Lord and my God!" and worshiped Him. Then Jesus told him, "Because you have seen me, you believed; blessed are those who have not seen, and yet believed."

The Purpose of John's Gospel

In fact, five hundred people saw Jesus risen from the dead. So, it is not only the disciples and a few women who saw him alive. But John wrote this record so that you may believe that Jesus is God's Anointed Chosen One, the Son of God, who is alive today, and by believing in Jesus, He is the KEY to eternal life in heaven.

God's peace be with you this Easter.

Discussion Questions

Q: In the story, what stood out to you for the first time?

Q: In this story, what is the main idea?

Q: What did you learn in the story about God, Jesus and/or yourself?

Q: If this story is true and what you have learnt from it is true, how will you live differently because of what you have learned from it?

Devotion

The Easter Story: Jesus' Crucifixion, Death, Burial, and Resurrection

ALONG THE CHRONOLOGICAL TIMELINE OF MATTHEW 27:31–61; LUKE 23:55–56; MAT-THEW 27:62–66; JOHN 20:1–29; 1 CORINTHIANS 15:6; JOHN 20:30–31.

The Easter story, the story of Jesus' crucifixion, death, burial, and resurrection is a major part of history. But there is a background leading up to this point. Why would Jesus go to all this trouble if there was not a problem with all humanity? This question can be clearly answered if we have a look at **the Bible Storyline of Sacrifice.**

Humanity's Problem and Need

At the dawn of time, before what we call "the Fall", Adam and Eve were in a right relationship with a good and holy God. But the moment they wanted to live separately from God, Adam and Eve's lives were forfeited because of their actions. The consequence for sin is death. Sin and brokenness came first, then death. Therefore, humanity's biggest problem is the brokenness of enjoying Gods resources (family, money, relationships, work, beaches, and parks), but living away from Him, and the wrath of God for living like this incurred. We are talking about the need for sacrifice.

Cain and Abel's sacrifice (Gen 4:1-26). Here God shows to us what may be the very fundamental concept related to sacrifice. "In sacrifice we offer back to God what is already his, by right" (Lawrence, 2010, p. 155).

Abraham, the sacrifice of his son Isaac (Gen 22:2). Once again, horrible as it sounds, the idea seems to be that of tribute and lordship. "It all belongs to God, and he has the right to take it back, even if it is your only son" (Lawrence, 2010, p. 155). At the last moment, God stops Abraham, and provides a ram (a male sheep) as an alternative sacrifice. "It turns out that God will accept a substitute for the life that is his to claim," and he will even provide the substitute (Lawrence, 2010, p. 156).

The Passover lamb (Ex 12). The Passover lamb was another sacrificial substitute. The year old male lamb "*without defect*" (Ex 12:5) was to be slaughtered and the blood was to be placed on "*the doorframes of the houses*" (Ex 12:7). After they roasted the meat and ate it as a Passover meal. When God saw the blood on the doorposts, he passed over them (Ex 12:13), and prevented the death of their first-born sons.

Leviticus sacrifices - The book of Leviticus is mainly about describing each of the various sacrifices that Israel had to offer God, as an atonement for their guilt and sin (Lawrence, 2010, p. 156). The sacrifices were repeated continuously year after year, but they never took away their guilt and sin (Heb 10:1–4). It was only a hint of what would come in Jesus Christ. On the cross, Jesus fulfilled everything the Old Testament sacrifice meant, and accomplished what they were unable to do.

Jesus and the Easter Story

So, according to Scripture, we do need a sacrifice. Jesus saw himself as the substitute (Erickson, 1985, p. 805). The one who came to die by offering himself to God, taking the punishment that his people deserved (Isa 53:4–6). "*The good shepherd lays down his life for the sheep*" (Jn 10:11). His sacrifice turned aside God's wrath and satisfied it. Jesus' sacrifice atones for our sin, removes the guilt that sin had incurred, making us at one with God (1 Jn 4:10) or right with God. This is where we get the word, righteousness.

The sacrifices described in Leviticus were repeated year after year, yet the book of Hebrews shows us Jesus was sacrificed once for all (Heb 7:27), by his own blood, to give us eternal rescue (Heb 9:12) and to take away our sin (Jn 1:29; Heb 9:26).

It turns out, the Old Testament sacrifices had only been a teaching aid, designed to lead us to Jesus. The good news is that on the cross Jesus accomplished salvation for those who listen to his call to turn back to God.

No More Sacrifice

Jesus calls us to pick up his cross and follow him (Lk 9:23) and offer ourselves as a living sacrifice (Rom 12:1–2). We are saved by faith alone, in Christ alone. There is no further sacrifice because Jesus the high priest of the new covenant is the last sacrifice that reconciles sinners to God. The idea of Jesus' sacrifice is that we might offer our lives back to God as an offering, not to pay for our sin, but as living sacrifices of praise to his glorious grace (Fry, p. 792).

The Emerging Lesson for Us

If we keep on offering these sacrifices as compensation for sin, to make God happy and to satisfy him, we will not succeed. But when we faithfully build up ourselves and others, showing that God is not furious any longer because Jesus has paid the penalty, something changes. Today, these living sacrifices are not presented in terror or worry, but in love. In one way, they are not really sacrifices at all. They are just proof of Jesus' love and being transformed to his image as a living sacrifice of praise to God's wonderful grace (Lawrence, 2010, p. 164).

The Emerging Question

Now that you have heard the Easter message and the Bible Storyline of Sacrifice. Do you understand and believe Jesus came to die as your substitute? As Jesus offered himself to God, taking the punishment that you and all humanity deserved. Because of all the years you spent using God's resources of life, relationships, food, money, the environment, but living at a distance from God.

Do you also understand and believe Jesus rose from the dead and is alive today? Because, if a person can do that, that is someone worth worshiping and following.

Do you choose His forgiveness as you turn back to God, living from now on closer to Him? Do you accept the call to follow Jesus? Becoming a disciple of Jesus, who learns to live like He did, as you walk and work along the disciple making path that he laid out for your life and for His mission through His teaching (Mt 28:19–20; Jn 13:15; 14:12; 17:4, 18; 20:21; Eph 3:10–11).

Will you love God and love other people as you connect your story to Jesus' story, which will give you a better end to your life story, forever? Then will you help connect others to Jesus' story, who go on connecting other people to Jesus' story, so we all can have a better end to our life stories? If yes, say the following prayer.

Prayer to Follow Jesus

Dear Lord Jesus, I know that I have lived my life at a distance from God, yet still receiving all the blessings from His resources, and I ask for your forgiveness. I believe Jesus died for my sins and rose from the dead. I turn back to God and invite you to be a part of my life. I want to trust and follow Jesus as my Lord and Savior as I connect my story line with Jesus' story line, for a better end to my life story.

Jesus, help me to stay connected to the people in this growth group, and into their story lines. Also, help me to connect to a place of worship where these people attend. So, I can continue to grow towards spiritual maturity over the coming years, as we all walk and work along the disciple making path that Jesus laid out for our lives and for His mission through His teaching.

Love you Jesus, and all the people said, "Amen," which means, "We all agree."

LEADERS' NOTES 1

A Disciple of Jesus is Someone who:

Has repented (Mt 4:17).

Has turned to the Lord (2 Cor 3:16).

Has the indwelling of the Holy Spirit (Cf. 2 Cor 3:17).

No longer lives for themselves but lives for Christ (2 Cor 5:15).

Is not worldly (2 Cor 5:16).

Is a new creation (2 Cor 5:17).

Is reconciled to Christ (2 Cor 5:18–20).

Has their sins removed (2 Cor 5:19).

Has been given the message of reconciliation (2 Cor 5:19).

Is an ambassador for Christ (2 Cor 5:20).

LEADERS' NOTES 2

Question 2

Being a Christian for many years, does not mean we are spiritually mature (see Hebrews 5:12-6:3). W.L. Lane, in his book, *A Call to Commitment,* on page 22 states, the "time period from the [Hebrews] conversion [to now in Hebrews 5:11] was a period of approximately 15 years." Yet within that time, one ought to be a teacher (Heb 5:12), someone who is spiritually mature, but they were not.

A period of 15 years is a reasonable time from conversion, to reach spiritual maturity, someone who can speak, tell, proclaim and teach the good news about Jesus and his disciple making path.

LEADERS' NOTES 3

Matthew 13:3-23

This parable is not just about the different responses to God's message, it is about the soil. The spiritual soil in most Western countries can be hard, so it needs to be prepared or cultivated for the seed. The seed needs to be sown at the right time in the right way, to produce an abundant harvest. It also needs the right soil conditions, such as good moisture and warmth. Cultivating the spiritual soil, planting the spiritual seeds in the right conditions, being ready for reaping the harvest and having labourers for the harvest (Lk 10:2; Mt 9:38) are all crucial parts of disciple making.

1. Move from **disconnecting** to **connecting** (Mt 13:3–24)
    Share to Win - Then Connect
    (Acts 14:21; Jn 17:4; Acts 2:42–47).

Jesus laid a foundation by cultivating the soil of relationships. He then invested in a few people by planting deep seeds of truth and finally reaping the harvest by mobilising them for outreach.

Cultivating: Breaking up the hardened ground involves prayer and becoming a friend of sinners.

Planting: Sowing seeds of truth at the right time and in the right way, are the keys to introducing God into a friendship.

Share: Disciples who follow Jesus, are transformed by him, and are committed to his mission, all purposefully building relationships with their non-Christian friends, those who are spiritually dead (Eph 2:1, 5). How? By sharing life together, having general conversations. Where? In relational environments. After having general conversations in relational environments, we eventually have spiritual conversations and invite them to hear the gospel message to *"come and see"* (Jn 1:39), to check out the facts about who Jesus is.

Reap - Bring in the harvest by clearly presenting the gospel and calling for a response.

Win: Win spiritually dead people for Jesus. As they respond and follow Jesus (spiritual rebirth), they become a spiritual infant who has put their faith in Jesus (becoming a disciple of Jesus), who follows him at the head level, is changed by Jesus at the heart level, and is committed to the mission of Jesus as disciple makers at the hands-on level (Mt 4:19). This occurs through reaching out to the community, making disciples who make other disciples, who move towards spiritual maturity (Mt 28:19–20).

Rally – Gather your ministry for broad seed sowing, resulting in an increase of new believers.

Connect: We help new disciples connect with other disciples (establishing ongoing relational connections) in relational environments. For example, having a coffee, (one-on-one or in a small group), or being involved in a church service or activity. These environments should concentrate on teaching people to obey the teaching of Jesus by building discipling relationships as Jesus did. Connecting them into biblical, relational environments, such as a Sunday morning church service (worship and community) and small groups (fellowship and support) is very important. We should teach them how to move towards spiritual maturity and disciple making (increasing new believers for Christ). When disciples have been nourished with spiritual food in these environments, they need spiritual exercise to keep growing (practicing disciple making) out into the wider community.

How will the soil affect the seed? We know that good soil opens doors to the gospel message. Remember it is Jesus that will convert them or win them. Our job is to share our life with them, eventually giving them an invitation to meet Jesus. Those who are converted to Christ are connected into small groups (biblical, relational environments).

LEADERS' NOTES 4

Spiritually Dead: Need to be reborn through Christ. Spiritual rebirth indicates becoming *"alive with Christ"*, having their sins forgiven (Col 2:13), by being *"born of God"* (Jn 1:13) into the family of God. Because they have move away from *"darkness [that had] blinded them"* (1 Jn 2:11), to the *"light"* where nothing can make them stumble (1 Jn 2:10).

Spiritual infant: Need to grow in their salvation. Grow by craving spiritual food, like milk that is easily digested. *"Like infants at the breast, drink deep of God's pure kindness. Then you'll grow up mature in God"* (1 Pt 2:2 MSG).

Spiritual children: Need to start making disciples. Even if it is just one step at a time or taking small steps at a time. Emphasis on the word, "start", to *"finishing the work [Jesus] gave [you] to do"* (Jn 17:4), which is the Great Commission of disciple making. Because **their** *"sins are forgiven in Jesus' name"* (1 Jn 2:12 MSG), and they *"know the Father from personal experience"* (1 Jn 2:13b MSG).

Spiritual young adults: Need to start looking after spiritual infant and child believers, like a babysitter or an older sidling. Because they have overcome the evil one and are strong and solid since the word of God remains in them. **Spiritual young people** *"such vitality and strength! God's word is so steady in you. Your fellowship with God enables you to gain a victory over the evil one"* (1 Jn 2:14b MSG).

Spiritually mature parent: Need to guide people towards maturity. By being a parent to spiritual infants and children. Because they know Jesus is the preexisting deity (1 Jn 2:13a, 14a) they gently comfort and encourage them *"like a [parent] caring for their little children"* (1 Thess 2:7, 12). Helping them to *drink deep of God's pure kindness [to] grow up mature in God"* (1 Pt 2:2 MSG) and teaching them to start *the* disciple making *work Jesus gave them to do* (Jn 17:4; Mt 28:19–20).

LEADERS' NOTES 4A

The purpose of these questions is, have you said any of these statements in the past and what spiritual stage is that. The hope is that the question would expose any false reality of someone thinking they are mature when they are just a spiritual child. Just because a person has been a Christian for 20 years does not necessary mean they are a mature believer. The intention is not to condemn the person but for them to identify the spiritual stage they are on, and then move towards spiritual maturity.

LEADERS' NOTES 5

Quiz Answers

Spiritual Child

How to help them:
- They need to learn to trust God obediently, doing what the Word says rather than what their feelings tell them to do.
- They need to learn to do the right things for the right reasons.
- They need to know what it means to have a servant heart, rather than one that is self-centered.

Spiritual Young Adult

How to help them:
- They need help identifying their gifts and receiving training in their areas of skill.

Spiritually Dead

How to help them:
- They need your prayers to soften their hearts. Pray for the harvest at 10.02am (as a reflection of Luke 10:2). Pray for people by name.

Spiritually Dead

How to help them:
- They need love through honest friendship and relationships with believers.

Spiritual parents

How to help them:
- They need permission to develop people to maturity.
- They need to be celebrated and honoured. What you celebrate, people will aspire to.

LEADERS' NOTES 6

Matthew 10:5–23

Training Workers

After months of intensive leadership training, Jesus sent out the twelve apprentices on their own mission trip. Jesus told them to take nothing, teaching them dependency on the Father. He sent them out just like the Father had sent Jesus out into the world, completely dependent on God for everything they would need.

Jesus even said, *"Do not worry about what to say or how to say it. At that time, you will be given what to say, for it will not be you speaking, but the Spirit of your Father speaking through you"* (Mt 10:19–20). Jesus also gave them instructions about how they were to enter the cities and villages and where they were supposed to go. This was a mission trip to the lost sheep of Israel (Mt 10:5–6), taking the gospel to their own people.

Jesus gave many more instructions on what house to enter, what to say, how long to stay and when to leave. He even instructed them on how to respond when they were persecuted for the message. Their short-term mission is like a training manual for us, showing us how to do short term missions within our own culture. The experience the disciples had in this situation was meant to teach the young leader's complete dependence on the Father. Six pairs of people went off on the adventure of a lifetime, taking the good news of God's kingdom and God's family to the lost Jewish people. This is what moving from informing people to preparing them looks like.

LEADERS' NOTES 7

Start Planning to Apply the Storytelling the Disciple Making Path

At this point, the small group leader is encouraged to pray and then plan to apply this material by storytelling Jesus' story. We suggest the small group leader be the first and the last person, on study 8 for the Christmas story and on study 16 for the Easter story. When the small group leader carries out the first storytelling, it will give the other group members an example and the confidence in the following weeks.

Feel free to look at the author's YouTube video, *Storytelling Jesus' Story - The Christmas Story* and other videos, as seen in Appendix 1. The videos cover the Easter story; Jesus' first followers; the lost animal, money, and the lost son; Jesus calms the storm and heals the demonic; Jesus, the blind man and Zacchaeus; Jesus heals the paralytic; Jesus heals the woman hemorrhaging for 12 years; Jesus is the Vine, we are the branches; Jesus is the way, the truth and the life. Please feel free to use any of these videos, especially if there is no one to do it that night or if someone scheduled to story tell becomes sick.

We also suggest the small group leader be the person leading the discussion time through studies 8 to 16. However, allowing someone else from the small group to lead the discussion time, two or three times, would be an effective way to encourage up-and-coming small group leaders.

As an Outreach

As an outreach, take a video of each story and post it on your Facebook page and ask the other small group members to share it with their Facebook friends. We hope and pray you will find the creative inspiration to undertake these videos, and may Jesus bless your prayerful efforts as you and your small group retells Jesus' stories, in his glorious name.

Also, as an outreach, the group could invite their friends over for a specific Storytelling Jesus' Story evening. This could happen at the normal mid-week time, or at some other time convenient for all. The Christmas and Easter celebrations could be a fantastic opportunity for non-church family and friends to hear the gospel. Start with a meal, then retell the story followed by discussion. Still take a video of the story and post it on your Facebook page, but do not record the discussion time.

Group Expectations During the Discussion Time

Follow the same group expectations as you would normally, however with the above outreach discussion time, it might be a good idea to briefly review them:

- Discussion questions have no right or wrong answers.
- Discussion time is on the story that was told on that night. Other questions outside the story can be followed up after the discussion time.
- In the discussion time, one person talks at a time - only one conversation at a time, please.
- If you are asked a question and you can't think of an answer, you can say "Pass". No one is going to make fun of that.

- Each person is encouraged to participate in the discussions, saying something briefly in order to give others the opportunity to have their say.
- Personal matters that are revealed in the group stays in the group. We must be able to trust one another to not spread personal stuff with others outside the group.
- Best of all, have some fun.

Discussion Questions

1. In the story, what did you notice for the first time or what stood out to you?
2. In this story, what is the main idea?
3. What does the story teach you about God, Jesus, and yourself?
4. If the story is true, how will you live differently because of what you have learnt from it?

Discuss the above questions as a group or in pairs or threes, for three minutes. This should encourage peer-to-peer conversations, eliminating any apparent teacher-student hierarchy. After, get them to share their answers with the whole group.

Very Important: The small group leader, the storyteller, and the Christians in the group, resist the temptation to comment on or summarize what non-Christian participants have said. Remember, it is about allowing people to say what they think, yet hear what the Christian say, and allow Jesus to do his work.

LEADERS' NOTES 8

Leadership Increase (Luke 10)

As the movement continued to grow, Jesus assembled the next set of leaders and appointed them in much the same way as he had with the twelve disciples. The seventy-two that he sent out were obviously disciples who had given up everything to follow Jesus and were now ready to be part of the growing leadership team. He called them together, gave them some final instructions and sent them on ahead of Him.

Jesus sent out the 72 in a similar way to the 12, with nothing on them so they could learn dependence on the Father. He wanted them to see that if they stepped out in faith, God would go before them and provide for everything they needed to complete the mission he had called them to. He wanted these new leaders to learn to walk by faith and not by sight. They moved as a great army of evangelists into the harvest fields. They were supposed to go to a village, find a man of peace and stay and minister from that person's house, heal the sick and tell them about the coming Kingdom of God. A person known as a person of peace (Lk 10:5) is key to making disciples, having influence through their hospitality and reputation. When they become disciples, they lead others to Christ.

It is important to know the 72 were commissioned to prepare the towns and villages for the coming visit by Jesus. This ministry served to prepare Israel for the official offer of its King in the triumphant entry into Jerusalem, which was less than six months away (Mt 21:1-17).

The 72 returned from their mission trip jumping up and down (Lk 10:20) and Jesus later broke into spontaneous praise to his Father (Lk 10:21).

The will of the Father was that Jesus would die on the cross, but the work of the Father was that Jesus would make disciples, who could make disciples, who could also make disciples. The work of making disciples who could make disciples was going to change the planet. That is what moving from accumulating numbers of people to sending them out, looks like.

Application

There is a joy that comes when you personally watch someone you have discipled come to Christ. Yet there is a deeper joy when many other disciples make other disciples. Because, now there are more who are glorifying God the Father, living in obedience to his will, dying to self, and doing Jesus' work of making disciples.

LEADERS' NOTES 9

Ephesians 4:11–16

God has given the church gifted ministry leaders, apostles, prophets, evangelists, pastors and teachers, mid-week bible study leaders, growth group leaders, youth leaders, Sunday school teachers and other ministry leaders. Why? To equip God's people for works of service, so that the community of Christ may be built up to maturity and *"to the whole measure of the fullness of Christ"* (Eph 4:13). Therefore, we must leave our spiritual immaturity behind. *"No more tossing back and forth or being blown here and there by every wind of teaching and by the cunning and craftiness of people in their deceitful scheming"* (Eph 4:14). Instead, share our experience of Jesus' love (share to win and then connect). This helps us to grow into a mature community of Christ. Study of the disciple making material in this study guide is a part of this maturity process and can be taught in a small group of new disciples. Leaders and teachers are God's spokespersons for his message to humanity. They are to nurture the flock, benefit the church, and unite people in faith, helping them grow towards spiritual maturity.

LEADERS' NOTES 10

Hebrews 5:11-6:12

Even though in the NIV it says, *"slow to learn"* (Heb 5:11), the Greek word is *nothros,* which is translated as lazy. The word "lazy" becomes the bookends that opens and closes the passage in Hebrews 5:11 & 6:12. It is a dangerous place to be if we are spiritually stagnant and lazy in our understanding.

William Lane in his book *A Call to Commitment,* has worked out that from the time of the Hebrews conversion in this part of the Bible passage, was approximately 15 years. Walking in your Christian life for 15 years is a typical period of time to reach some sort of spiritual maturity. As an infant and child believer, we feed on the milk of the foundations of God's word: which are, repentance, faith or belief in God, teaching about baptism, laying on hands (receiving the Holy Spirit, healing, blessing), the resurrection, and eternal life.

Now let us build on this foundation, a spiritual life that is sustained by the solid food of sound doctrine, with its protection and spiritual discernment. All this helps us to take action and grow in our faith in Jesus and mature spiritually, to avoid, *"falling away"* (Heb 6:6), to be *"diligent to the end"* (Heb 6:11) and not to be lazy or slow to learn these things (Heb 6:12).

LEADERS' NOTES 11

Q: In what other ways does Jesus control the environment?

A: Walks on water, changes water to wine, feeds five thousand people with a boy's lunch, transfigures, rises from the dead.

Q: What do you think about the idea that evil tried to stop Jesus coming to Decapolis (a predominant Gentile region)? Therefore, who starts storms (God or the devil)?

A: In no way is God and the devil equal. In Job's story (Job 1:6-2:10), the devil does roam the earth trying to find someone to destroy. It is only with God's permission that the devil can inflict scores onto Job, but he must spare his life (Job 2:6). We understand that God's permission is to show the devil that Job won't curse God. It would seem that the devil can start *"a great wind"* (Job 1:19), but it's only by God's permission. All that Job went through, the loss of his business, his family, and his home. At the end, God gave back to Job *"twice as much as he had before"* (Job 42:10). The devil might be able to start a storm to try and stop Jesus going to the other side of the lake, but Jesus has the power to calm the storm.

Q: If a person is not for Jesus, by default they are serving the Inner-Critic (the devil), which might be some form of evil possession, or they live in fear of evil spirits (hearts are hard and ears don't want to hear, because of the devil's influence)? So, how much influence does the inner critic have on average Christian?

A: See the discussion notes in Study 13 on shrink or starve the Inner Critic.

Q: Why would Jesus forbid some people to speak about being
healed and in this situation say, "Go tell everyone"?

A: In this half-heathen region, the Jewish opposition is non-existent
and there is no other missionary in that area.

LEADERS' NOTES 12

Write and Speak Out Loud These Following Statements Five or Six Times.

Acknowledge, and Resolve

First, we need to acknowledge the issue and resolve them. If we do not acknowledge (anger, anxiety, feeling down, worry or fear), we cannot move forward to resolution, because the Inner Critic will keep the lie going as long as we let him.

Therefore, the issue or lies needs to be resolved. We resolve these issues or lies by writing and speaking out loud, true statements, five or six times.

Some Examples of True Statements

Mr Smith (the person's name), said I am immature (or some other untrue statement), and it hurt me very deeply.

Mr Smith is human, he is not perfect, and he makes mistakes, just like me and everybody else.

When I came to this place (name of church, workplace etc.), no one gave them a book on how to treat me.

This anger (or anxiety, feeling down, worry or fear), does not belong to me and it is not good for me or anyone else.

My family loves me very much and they want the very best for me.

Because of this anger (or anxiety, feeling down, worry or fear), I have now decided to let all the anger (or anxiety, feeling down, worry or fear) go.

Because of this stuff, I have now decided to brush off all of the stuff (the anger, anxiety, feeling down, worry or fear), that does not belong to me. (Use a brushing action, as if brushing something off your arm, waist, and legs.)

Say out loud the above truth statements frequently. Inside of us the change happens automatically. Statements such as these, said repeatedly, automatically change the neural pathways which *change our behavior.* This is a God given ability to transform our mind, as Romans 12:2 states, "Let's *be transformed by the renewing of your mind*". Yes, this really works, what do you have to lose?

This works because these WORDS are true, and the truth will set you free (Jn 8:32). If they are not working all that good, repeat true WORD statements, another five to six times. Also, repeat these true WORD statements whenever anger, anxiety, feeling down, worry or fear arises.

Note: You are not going to be able to fully remove these nasty emotions, because they are a part of your personality. But it could take approximately three to four months to feel in control of these emotions. It's the control we are looking for, *"be angry, but don't sin"* (Eph 2:26). It's OK to be angry, but to have control is a wonderful thing. I personally have been placed into some horrible situations, where I could have easily lost it (became angry). But as I have driven home, I have even surprised myself, I didn't get angry.

Remember, these *TRUE WORDS* build up a defence that *shrinks* and *starves* the Inner Critic, which is based on Garfield Thompson's, *Neuroplasticity Therapy,* 2019.

APPENDIX 1

The Author's Videos on Storytelling Jesus' Stories

The Story Behind This Book

Phillip Matthews, (2023, Apr 10), *The story behind the book "Storytelling the Disciple Making Path"* [Video]. YouTube.
https://www.youtube.com/watch?v=ev2HqxtBZUo&t=44s

The Outline for this Book

Phillip Matthews, (2024, Mar 28), *An Outline for the Book, "Storytelling the Disciple Making Path"* [Video]. YouTube.
https://www.youtube.com/watch?v=R88AJcqBIIo

Please Note : Some videos were not available at the time of this print. However, they may be recorded after. So please check the authors YouTube videos @phillipmatthews9015

Study 8: The Christmas Story: God has Moved into the Neighbourhood

Matthews, P, (2021, Dec 23), Storytelling Jesus' Story - The Christmas Story [Video]. YouTube.
https://www.youtube.com/watch?v=9byoHAcJS-8&t=97s

Study 9: Jesus First Followers: Come, See and Follow Jesus

Matthews, P, (2022, Mar 21), *Storytelling Jesus' Story - Jesus First Followers* [Video]. YouTube.
https://www.youtube.com/watch?v=XKszyCVPA4E&t=7s

Study 10: The Lost Animal, the Lost Money and the Lost Son

Matthews, P, (2022, Mar 22), Storytelling Jesus' Story - The lost animal, coin and the lost son [Video]. YouTube.

https://www.youtube.com/watch?v=mSjx9fcSv0M&t=202s

Study 11: The Blind Man and Zacchaeus

Matthews, P, (2022, Jun 11), Storytelling Jesus' Story - Jesus the Blind Man and Zacchaeus [Video]. YouTube.

https://www.youtube.com/watch?v=PoN7HzAlQ4g&t=104s

Study 12: Jesus Heals the Paralytic: Forgiveness

Matthews, P, (2022, Jul 9), *Storytelling Jesus' Story - Jesus Heals the Paralytic* [Video]. YouTube.
https://www.youtube.com/watch?v=tXqsEr-agbE&t=50s

Study 13: Jesus Calms the Storm and Heals the Demonic: Heals and Restores

Matthews, P, (2022, May 14), Storytelling Jesus' Story - Jesus Calms the Storm and Heals the Demonic [Video]. YouTube.
https://www.youtube.com/watch?v=dMWeOpiPfok

Study 14: Jesus Heals the Women Hemorrhaging for 12 years

Matthews, P, (2022, Aug 13), Storytelling Jesus' Story - Jesus Heals the Women Hemorrhaging for 12 years [Video]. YouTube.
https://www.youtube.com/watch?v=PtHu7psfktU&t=20s

Study 15: Jesus is the Only Trustworthy Path to Heaven

Matthews, P, (2022, Sep 10), *Storytelling Jesus' Story - Jesus is the way, the truth and the life* [Video]. YouTube.
https://www.youtube.com/watch?v=MTmzjqiPa6s&t=112s

Study 16: The Easter Story: Jesus' Crucifixion, Death, Burial, and Resurrection

Matthews, P, (2022, Apr 9), *Storytelling Jesus' Story - The Easter Story* [Video]. YouTube. https://www.youtube.com/watch?v=FYTSylCV1f4&t=26s

The Author's Personal Testimony

Phillip Matthews, (2023, Jun 12), Phil's personal testimony of following Jesus [Video]. YouTube. https://www.youtube.com/watch?v=QOa0jlQ3jtM&t=56s

BIBLIOGRAPHY

According to the New York Times, *"Jesus the most significant person in all history,"* cited from Faase, K, (2016, June 29). *Jesus the Game Changer* [Video]. YouTube. https://www.youtube.com/watch?v=AtyvHebPoqY

Audi, R., 1995, 'Postmodern', *The Cambridge Dictionary of Philosophy*, Cambridge University Press, Cambridge.

Bennett, M., 2004, *Christianity Explained*, DVD, Scripture Union. https://www.abundantlifechristianbookstore.com.au/brand/scripture-union/

Benson, D., 2024, 12 April, *Discipleship in a Digital Age*, Blog, https://lausanne.org/report/digital-ministry/discipleship

Bloesch, D.G., 'Sin. The Biblical Understanding of', in Elwell, W.A. 1984, *Evangelical Dictionary of Theology*, Baker Books, Grand Rapids, p. 1012.

Butler, S., Ed., 2009, 'Democracy', *Macquarie Concise Dictionary*, (5th ed), Macquarie Dictionary Publishers, Sydney, p. 329.

Cox, S.L. & Easley, K.H. 2007, *Harmony of the Gospels*, Holman, Nashville.

Chan, S., 2018, *Evangelism in a Skeptical World: How to make the unbelievable news about Jesus more believable*, Zondervan, Grand Rapids.

Chan, S., 2020, *How to Talk About Jesus: Without Being that Guy*, Zondervan, Grand Rapids.

Chamblin, J.K. 'Matthew', cited in Elwell, W.A. 1996, *Evangelical Commentary on the Bible*, (4th ed), Baker Books, Grand Rapids, pp. 719-760.

Edwards, M., 2010, *Knowing Him: A 50-day study in the life of Christ*, Campus Crusade for Christ, Sydney.

Erickson, M.J. 1985, *Christian Theology*, Baker Books, Grand Rapids.

Elwell, W.A. 1996, *Evangelical Commentary on the Bible*, (4th ed), Baker Books, Grand Rapids.

Elwell, W.A. 1984, *Evangelical Dictionary of Theology*, (12th ed), Baker Books, Grand Rapids.

Faase, K., *Jesus the Game Changer* – Olive Tree Media. www.olivetreemedia.com.au/jesus-the-game-changer/

Faase, K., 2016, *Jesus the Game Changer* DVD, https://olivetreemedia.com.au

Faase, K., (2016, June 29). *Jesus the Game Changer* [Video]. YouTube. https://www.youtube.com/watch?v=AtyvHebPoqY

Faase, K., 2016, *Jesus the Game Changer, How the Life and teaching of Jesus Changed the World and Why it Matters, Discussion Guide*, Olive Tree Media, Sutherland, NSW.

Faase, K, (2017, June 9). *How did Jesus treat women? Jo Vitale on Jesus the Game Changer* [Video]. YouTube. *https://www.youtube.com/watch?v=Hu-egO1ueP4*

Faase, K., (2019, Aug 9). *Jesus the Game Changer Season 2 – Trailer* [Video]. YouTube. https://www.youtube.com/watch?v=y9w0NMdWjJg

FactChecker: *Divorce Rate Among Christians - The Gospel Coalition,* (2012, Sep 25), sighted on (2018, Feb 7).

Finkelde, J., (2022), *5 Simple Things Unhealthy Churches Never Measure,* [Blog]. Grow a Healthy church. https://www.growahealthychurch. com/5-simple-things-unhealthy-churches-never-measure/ https://www.thegospelcoalition.org/article/ factchecker-divorce-rate-among-christians/

Kennedy, D.J. 1983, *Evangelism Explosion,* (3rd ed), Adept Printing, Bankstown.

Kimball, D., 2008, *They like Jesus but not the Church: Participant's Guide,* Zondervan, Grand Rapids.

Fry, C.G., 'Offerings and Sacrifices in Bible Times,' in Elwell, W.A. 1984, *Evangelical Dictionary of Theology,* (12th ed), Baker Books, Grand Rapids, pp. 788-793.

Harm, F.R. 'Sin. Mortal', in Elwell, W.A. 1984, *Evangelical Dictionary of Theology,* (12th ed), Baker Books, Grand Rapids, p. 1016.

Harrison, E.F. 'Apostle, Apostleship', in Elwell, W.A. 1984, *Evangelical Dictionary of Theology,* (12th ed), Baker Books, Grand Rapids, pp. 70-72.

Holdsworth, W., 1649, 'A History of English Law', Cited in Zimmermann, A., July 2024, 'Constituting a Christian Commonwealth – A Quarterly Essay on Important Social and Political Issues', *MainPoint – Family Voice Australia,* pp. 1-4.

Johnson, T.F. 1993, *New International Biblical Commentary; 1, 2, 3 John,* Zondervan, Grand Rapids.

Lawrence, M., 2010, *Biblical Theology in the Life of the Church: A Guide for Ministry,* Crossway, Illinois.

Matthews, P.G. 2007, *Case Study: Church Health and Patterns of Growth (and or decline) Over the Past Five Years.* Subject Unit, "Church Dynamics & Growth," B.Min, Vose Seminary, Western Australia.

Matthews, P.G. 2009, *Evangelism in the Postmodern Context,* Subject Unit "6,000-word Research Essay", Grad Dip.Min, Vose Seminary, Western Australia.

Matthews, P.G. 2017, *Being in God's Family Solves our Identity and Sin Crises: An Essay in 1 John 2:28-3:10.* Subject Unit, "14,000-word Research Essay", Master of Arts (Biblical Studies), Sydney College of Divinity at Perth Bible College, Western Australia.

Matthews, P.G. (2022, Nov 12), *Storytelling Jesus' Story - The Persistent Widow Pray don't give up* [Video]. YouTube. https://www.youtube.com›watch

Matthews, P.G. (2022, Apr 9), *Storytelling Jesus' Story - The Easter Story* [Video]. YouTube. https://www.youtube.com›watch

May, S., 'Missiological Concepts in the Gospels', cited in Cox, S.L. & Easley, K.H. 2007, *Harmony of the Gospels,* Holman, Nashville, p. 342.

Moran, R., (2014, Oct 8) *What are disciple making movements,* [Video]. YouTube. http://www.disciplekc.com

McAlpine, S., 2022, *Being the Bad Guy: How to live for Jesus in a world that says you shouldn't,* The Good Book Company, Stanmore.

Munn, M., 2016, Cited from sermon at Woodvale Baptist Church.

North, J., 2010, *Growth Works: Helping You Back onto the Path of Spiritual Growth*, DVD, EvangelismShift, afci.com.au

North, J., 2015 *EvangelismShift* seminar, at Woodvale Baptist Church.

North, J., 2015, *LifeWorks: Walking with People Towards Christ*, DVD, https://afci.com.au

Powers, W.B., 2010, *The Progressive Publication of Matthew: An Explanation of the Writing of the Synoptic Gospels*, B&H Publishing Group, Nashville.

Putman, J., (2008, Jan 18). *Church Is a Team Sport* [Video]. *YouTube.* https://www.youtube.com/watch?v=AtbRc1-ynKI

Putman, J., & Harrington, B., 2013, *DiscipleShift: Five steps That Help your Church make Disciples who make Disciples*, Zondervan, Grand Rapids.

Putman, J., (2015, Jan 1), Evangelism vs. Discipleship [Video]. YouTube. https://www.youtube.com/watch?v=-UW51X8fOgU

Rayburn R.S., 'Christians, Names of,' cited in Elwell, W.A. 1984, *Evangelical Dictionary of Theology*, (12th ed), Baker Books, Grand Rapids, pp. 216-218.

Richardson, R., 2000, *Evangelism Outside the Box: New ways to help people experience the Good News*, IVP, Downers Grove.

Schreiner, T.R., 'Luke', cited in Elwell, W.A. 1996, *Evangelical Commentary on the Bible*, (4th ed), Baker Books, Grand Rapids, pp. 799-839.

Sessoms, R., (2012, April 12), *Telling the Gospel Story: The Great Commission to Oral learners*, [Blog]. Freedom to Lead, https://freedomtolead.net › telling-story-great-commission-oral-learners/

Shelton, R.L., 'Perfection', cited in Elwell, W.A. 1984, *Evangelical Dictionary of Theology*, (12th ed), Baker Books, Grand Rapids, p. 839.

Spader, D., 2012, *Movement Building: from the life of Christ*, Power to Change, Sydney.

Spiceland, J.D., 'Miracles', in Elwell, W.A. 1984, *Evangelical Dictionary of Theology*, (12th ed), Baker Books, Grand Rapids, p. 723.

Stark, R., 1996, *The Rise of Christianity*, Harper One, San Francisco.

Thomas, R.L. & Gundry, S.N. 1998, *The NIV Harmony of the Gospels*, Harper Collins, New York.

Thompson, G., 2019, *Neuroplasticity Therapy*.

Unknown author., (2022, Apr 23), *On My Father's Side* – The Village Singers [Video]. YouTube. https://www.youtube.com › watch

Unknown author., (2013, Dec 11), *3, 2, 1, You, the world and God* [Video]. YouTube. http://three-two-one.org.

Westlake, G, 23 June 2024, Sermon, *Foundations of the Christian Worldview*, presented at Woodvale Baptist Church.

Youngblood, R., 'Judgment,' in Elwell, W.A. 1984, *Evangelical Dictionary of Theology*, (12th ed), Baker Books, Grand Rapids, pp. 590-591.

Zimmermann, A., July 2024, 'Constituting a Christian Commonwealth – A Quarterly Essay on Important Social and Political Issues', *MainPoint – Family Voice Australia*, pp. 1-4.

ALSO, BY PHILLIP G. MATTHEWS

Storytelling Jesus' Story

16 Studies for Individuals or Groups

ISBN 978-1-92388-50-4 (paperback) 143 pages
ISBN 978-1-923156-05-0 (eBook)

Bible Study Guide

We all love to hear a great story and if speaking God's Word is the only primary pursuit in sharing our faith in Jesus. One brilliant way of doing this is **Storytelling Jesus' Story**, which offers a better ending to everybody's story.

Storytelling the Act of the Apostles

16 Studies for Individuals or Groups

ISBN 978-1-923265-38-7 (paperback) 175 pages
ISBN 978-1-923386-09-9 (eBook)

Bible Study Guide

I hope this material will help you rethink about new opportunities to witness for Christ, and I dearly hope this would encourage you to video your storytelling. Video Storytelling is the best and greatest tool in our lifetime. It helps us to compel others towards Jesus, because today there really is a great need and hope for a reliable picture of what disciple making looks like through Storytelling the Acts of the Apostles.

ebooks and paperback copies are available from your local Christian bookshop, online bookstores, or email: *sales.storytellingthedmp@gmail.com*